Celebr ‖‖‖‖‖‖‖‖‖‖‖‖

Diversity

Sharing stories of Migration

Compiled and Edited by

Amina Chitembo

Diverse Cultures Publishing

Authors: Amina Chitembo | Angelinah Boniface | Charity Ngugi-Latz
Ali Abdoul | Clara Meierdierks | Judita Grubliene | Bernadetta Omondi
Savithri Jayaweera | Roland Burt |Lucy Oyubo |

Published by Diverse Cultures Publishing, UK

Layout: Amina Chitembo and the Diverse Cultures Squad.

Cover Graphics: Ahsan Chuhadry

Paperback ISBN: 978-0-9957396-8-0

Dedications

To all who appreciate differences and enjoy living in a world where inclusion is the driving force to development.

Contents

Introduction

By Amina Chitembo

"Diversity, inclusion, engagement and meaningful social mixing are terms that you will come across in today's world. Can we truly exist without differences."

Celebrating Diversity book is the second anthology in Diversity Series, written by ten authors from different countries and published by Diverse Cultures Publishing. A company I founded to help people who want to share their message with the world but find it difficult to do so in the traditional publishing space.

This book brings together exciting stories from people from different backgrounds who share their experiences of what truly 'Celebrating Diversity' means to them. The book is packed full of outright factual personal encounters which are set in a humorous way by ten authors from around the world. The purpose of the book to share experience, enlighten and to teach something new to the readers of the book.

WHY THIS BOOK AND WHY NOW

"Celebrating Diversity"

I start this book of with my take on celebrating diversity. I see people every day and each one of us different and yet we can all sit on a room and produce marvellous results.

I took interest in the subject of meaningful engagement, diversity and inclusion when I moved from Zambia to the United Kingdom in 2001. I arrived with no thought that someone like me would be considered different from the next person and be offered different opportunities.

The terms ethnic minority and disadvantaged became common place for me and some of the people around me. This raised my curiosity to a point that I wanted to help the community that I was now living in to become better at dealing with diverse communities. The stories that have been shared in this book will enrich the conversation and finding of the solutions people seek in understanding how when we just ask and get to understand one another, we would be more welcoming and more helpful to those who do not look like us and those who do not act or walk like us.

Diversity can be described in many different ways. Academics have researched some the advantages and disadvantages of falling into one or more of Diversity categories. My research has at times thrown up more questions than answers about what Diversity is and how many types of Diversity exist. There are the main characteristics of what is already known, the one I call visible diversity; then there is the hidden diversity. All these come down to the importance of our understanding that we are all unique, and recognising those individual differences. These differences come in the dimensions of race, ethnicity, gender, sexual orientation, socio-economic status, age, physical abilities, religious beliefs, political beliefs, or other ideologies.

Here I will share the different types I have come to learn about The visible Diversity dimensions are pretty much self-explanatory and are more commonly referred to in inclusion conversations. I will not go into details to explain these, but if you wish to find out more, please contact me. Alternatively searching the internet will bring up sites where the details are given. The subject is very wide I will spend less time in this book about the definitions.

Visible Diversity
  Visible Diversity includes:
  - all forms of physical and mental disability Diversity
  - race and race-related Diversity
  - Sexuality Diversity
  - Faith, religious and non-religious Diversity
  - Gender Diversity
  - Age Diversity

Invisible Diversity

Invisible Diversity Includes:

Neuro Diversity - Neurodiversity is related to mental and neurological differences. Some scientists argue that neurological conditions are the result of normal variations in the human genome and have challenged to prevailing views of neurological diversity as inherently unreasonable or difficult. Some examples of Neurally Diverse people include a person with Dyslexia like me, Aspergers Syndrome, OCD and many other conditions where people do not follow the set 'norm' or pattern of behaviour.

Self Diversity – has to do with each one of us understanding ourselves through self-refection and self-awareness. We are all unique and individual, understanding ourselves will help us deal with situations we face and appreciate the people we come in contact more as being unique and different from us but nonetheless.

Situational Diversity – We all act differently depending on the situation we find ourselves in. In the simplest form, this has to do with the way we behave towards other people who are of the same social class would be different from the way we behave when we find people of a different class. It can also be a question of circumstances dictating our behaviour. Many women will tell you about how isolated they feel once they have had a baby. Their situation moves from being able to do what everyone else is doing to having to think of another people, of course the bundle of joy before making any move. This situation, however, does not last a lifetime you may be aware. It is temporary but can have huge consequences and can be life-altering.

Personality Diversity – Myrs Briggs, Disc and many similar tools have been used for years to try and read people's personalities. We are all different, and one may fall on into one or more personality categories. There some people though who refuse to be pigeonholed into personality Diversity categories. Any employer will tell you that there certain types of people who will work together better than other types.

Socio-economic Diversity – This has to do with social-economic status. The diversity we experience in the developed world is different from that experienced in the third world. People working in the same organisation coming from different socio-economic backgrounds will behave differently even when though education they have ended up with the same time of job and earn the same amount of money.

These are just a few ways in which we can dice and slice diversity. This book is more about experiences rather than definitions. People in both categories experience disparities in accessing services, receiving compensation for services provided, and most importantly functioning as a unit to move themselves forward in life.

The bottom line is that we are all different and that is what makes the world a beautiful place. Wher these diversity dimensions are celebrated people are happier, communities are stronger, and there is more inclusion.

The big question is; What would the world be like if we were all the same? I will leave you to answer this question,

THE RICHNESS OF DIALECTS
AND DIVERSE ENGLISH ON THE STREET

The authors of this book have all diverse in their background vocabulary, educational attainment and country of residence. They come with the richness of writing and speaking in more than one language. These are real stories, and people have used their day to day English, which may seem wrong to some readers. The aim is not to have a polished book but one that introduces you to the life of the author in their language, vocabulary, and richness of the everyday words that they use. If you are looking for 'native

English' perfection, you will not find it in this book. We made a conscious decision to ignore the Oxford, Cambridge, Harvard or any other English rule and instead showcase the way we speak in the day to day life. It is my sincere hope that you will enjoy and learn how beautiful the variety of language and sentence formulation is when you are not a so-called native English speaker. Even a person like me who was born in a British Colony and pretty much spoke English from the day I learned how to speak.

The correct English was drummed into me in School, arriving in the UK was a shock because I have moved from South to North and West to East and pronunciations and vocabulary vary enormously. For that reason alone, it impossible to know how correct English sounds. In addition to that, the generation we live in now, new words are coming up. English is constantly getting a squeeze as it gets mixed with diverse dialects, text speech and other forms of simplifying communication.

The composition in this book is fun, and we love it. We hope you will love it too. The authors make no apologies for who they are and have chosen to embrace that in this book.

It is our aim that you will enjoy the book without frustration about word placements and grammar. The best efforts have gone into the production of this masterpiece; however, it is not perfect, and as the publisher, I do not want it to be perfect. I represent a diverse range of people who write from the heart. This book is written and produced in an imperfectly perfect way. It is not an academic book it is instead a factual account of real people with real-life stories, sharing their real-life experiences and accounts. As such I do not advocate for perfectionism because I have a strong belief that most of world's problems and lack of education are perpetuated by the insistence of grammar that is based on only the 'correct' English. The English that people speak on the streets and not from a textbook. Equally, as a dyslexic, no matter how much I read this book I am about to make a mistake. I do not want to be judged by that, the same for my fellow authors in my book series.

However, if you find an error that is entirely unacceptable, please email us, and we will be review it and we will possibly amend it in subsequent editions.

I thank you, dear reader, for your support by buying and reading this book. I am sure you will find very intriguing and educative.

Please buy some copies for your loved ones too. The proceeds go a long way in spreading the message of the positive stories of diversity.

STEPPING OUT OF THE COMFORT ZONE TO LEAD

"Looking for a Black African woman.
You are dull; you don't check your work"

In 2005, I was working for the health service when I was called upon a commissioner to lead a project to teach Africans in my County how not to spread HIV. He asked me to consider it because they had been 'looking for a Black African woman' to lead the project alongside a Black African man who had already been found and employed.

That was the point at which I first took note that I was different, and I had certain 'super powers' as a black woman. He approached me after he had heard about my previous experience working in a London School of Hygiene and Tropical Medicine funded HIV and Tuberculosis Research organisation in my native country, Zambia.

I quickly jumped at this opportunity partly because it was more money despite it being a one-year project initially and for once non-UK work experience was not a disadvantage.

Secondly, I wanted to make a difference as I was not very happy in my health service job teaching people how to use computers.

I had experienced, and observed instances where the difference between 'normal' and 'disadvantaged' people were so apparent that if you experienced any of the following, you will treat them differently but complaining would sometimes mean more trouble: your race, disability, older or younger, religion or belief or sexual orientation.

To me, the thought of teaching 'black people to stop spreading HIV', gave me a lot of questions. I wanted the opportunity to help both my community and the policy makers. It highlighted the lack of sensitivity, lack of concept on how to go about solving global problem, and the sheer chance to be part of the leadership to this problem. Besides, I had already lost many of my own family members to the HIV/AIDS scourge, nonetheless that is a story for another day. Here, I am concentrating on Diversity and Inclusion. In particular celebrating Diversity.

The one year project led to me setting up a charitable company which was a consultancy for mainstream organisations wanting to be more inclusive to Ethnic Minority communities or disadvantaged communities and also to give the opportunity to the less disadvantaged to participate more fully in society, by helping them to solve their problems such as language barriers, i.e. teaching them English, escaping domestic abuse, dealing with disability access, LGBT/ethnic minority issues and even mental health. I did the work for ten years, and in that time I learned more than I had bargained for, and went on to achieve a Masters Degree in Leadership and Management with a with a focus on Transformation, Diversity and Inclusion in Organisations and public life. I also burned out in the process because I realised that I had built a level of dependency. I would do it differently now believe me!

Even as I performed at a high level in various leadership forums, and sat made a difference, managed to write successful funding bids. There was still one problem though; my work was never perfect or error-free. To some extent, I can say I am lucky most people see beyond the typos. I avoided reading in public at all costs. Shhhhhh… I can't read fluently!

Then in 2015, I went back into the health service at a much more senior level now. I could produce great reports and business cases, however, as there was no one readily waiting to help me check the spellings of my work, and I had deadlines to meet. I went through hell with a manager that made sure I was marked down for every letter I missed. My condition which at that point I didn't know that it was even a thing, now I know it is Dyslexia had not been diagnosed.

This took me back to those years in primary school when the teacher would humiliate me in front of the class because I couldn't not read and write as well as the other kids in the class. When all my young cousins, nephews and nieces could easily read like they were news readers, and all I could do was go and hide each time someone even mentioned reading.

This experience ate away at my self-esteem and caused me to dread going into work. Until, I decided to speak workplace emotional wellbeing team. They were very helpful, and they referred me to see a psychotherapist.

It was through these sessions that I was asked if I had been checked for Dyslexia. *"Dys what???"* I found myself asking… It only took 42 years to find that I had this thing? So yes, there are many people who struggle with dyslexia. By the way Dyslexia in case you don't know about it yet;

Dyslexia is a common learning difficulty that can cause problems with reading, writing and spelling. It's a specific learning difficulty, which means it causes problems with certain abilities used for learning, such as reading and writing. Unlike a learning disability, intelligence is not affected. Source: Dyslexia – NHS.

In the developed worlds, it can be picked up quickly, where I grew up, it was a question of survival of the fittest, so no help came my way. People suffer different levels of dyslexia, mine is quite high, so it can't just be brushed under the carpet.

The discovery as I call it now has made me more determined to do the same things that my brain misfires. It is not a joke, but I think it is laughable when we have to get labels to start changing the status quo.

To set the tone of the book, I have started with talking about Diversity, in general, to give an idea that even if the authors talk about their experience regarding migration. I want to ensure that we do not miss the fact that Diversity goes beyond racial divides. It is a far wider topic than we can cover in one book, so for the purposes of this book, we write in greater part about the positive stories of migration from around the world. It is after all the sticking point when people are not happy with where they are living. It is the migrants that cause problems according them; it is the migrants that have changed our way of life. These perceptions have a tendency of masking the real issues that cause people to behave in a way that excludes those who are seen as 'not part of us'.

EXPERIENCES AND DIVERSITY

My own situations and meeting other people along my professional journey has made me rethink the focus of any Diversity and Inclusion training or agendas that are out there. I find that if we do not help more people who are otherwise excluded. Excluded from performing to the best of their strengths simply because they do not fit the 'norm', we are missing out on celebrating the diversity that the universe has bestowed upon us. So I took a stance to help myself firstly. I started by picking up on my writing. Some work I had done which was just gathering dust in my hard drive as

I lived in fear of being judged and humiliated, I turned the work into books and stories. Next, I stepped out into the public calling myself the 'Happily Imperfect Leader'. You will find that this the title of some of my ventures such as my blog, youtube channel and SoundCloud/iTunes. This was for me a defining moment to tell anyone who did not accept me with my neurally diverse brain, wasn't welcome to sit on my table.

I discovered that I was dyslexic around December 2015, The process to reinvent myself started in October 2016, On February 2017, I launched myself as Diversity and Inclusion Coach and Book Writing coaching. I left my well-paid job in the health service and decided to start this business to help other people just like me, find themselves and gain confidence to be who they are.

The journey has been an exciting challenge, I have at times thought I am crazy because my family has gone on the minimum as mummy tries to build and grow this business. A lot of work has gone in and alas the results are now showing.

I love living in a world that is so diverse that everything goes and as long as no one is killing another person, we can all celebrate our differences. Rather than being so judgemental of others, and don't get me wrong, I do it too. That is because I am imperfect. We all have a certain level of bias. What matters is how we use that for good. We identify it, acknowledge it and then do the right thing.

For instance; If women are not sitting in the boardrooms of the fortune 500 companies, the question ought to be, how can we make sure that more women are trained, advised, and encouraged to apply for those positions. Rather than labelling the boards as 'white men's clubs.

If we all see someone who doesn't quite fit in at team parties and doesn't join the after-work drinks, how can we bring the fun to where they are. It is far better than labelling them as non-team players.

If an immigrant starts working in your organisation, how can you make sure that it is the job of the rest of the team to welcome that person and make friends with them even if they look and dress differently? Instead of thinking the person is happy to be left on their own, make them a friend.

We all love restaurant food. It is good to have someone else make the dinner, and I go and sit down to eat. But how about if we have more restaurants that offer foods from different countries in one place so that families do not have to be forced to choose between a Chinese, Indian or Mexican restaurant. I know there are a few of these types of restaurants popping up but more will be better, so that food diversity and inclusion become common place.

It is the simple things that add up and make a big difference. So let us start where we are. Let us all practice some **Kaizen, or the one-minute principle** towards Celebrating Diversity

In Japanese culture, there exists the practice of **Kaizen**, which includes the idea of the 'one-minute principle' for self-improvement. At the heart of this method is the idea that a person should practice doing something for a single minute, every day at the same time. - Various sources.

Enjoy the rest of the book.

Judita Grubliene

Judita Grubliene, Outreach Project Officer, Peterborough Museum. Lay Member of Peterborough Child Safeguarding Board for East Europeans of Peterborough and Cambridgeshire. Poet. Editor of Magazine Lighthouse (2010-2015). Teacher of Peterborough Lithuanian Saturday School "Amber". Chair of Peterborough Lithuanian Community Lighthouse. Ethnology and Lithuanian Philology bachelor's degree, Klaipeda University, Lithuania.

Books and Publications:
  Poetry book - At the Gates of Nonexistence, 2010
  Magazine – Svyturys (Lighthouse), 2010 – 2015

Contact Details:
  www.svyturys.org
  https://www.facebook.com/Svyturys-Peterborough-73605
4243170796/
  https://www.facebook.com/judita.gru

Turning Challenges Into Opportunities

By Judita Grubliene

Bridging communities with cultural events, connecting people, and spreading the word through poetry. For me, poetry is high pilotage of words, haute couture of meanings.

My passion is to recognise the uniqueness of creativity of each one person I am communicating with and direct that creativity together in all ways into high-level outcomes. Looking back, I am wondering how many wonderful people I've met in my life, and how much amazing things we've created together.

But, the most beautiful things in life are not things – they're people and places, and memories, and pictures. They're feelings and moments and smiles and laughter.

Miracles happen when we accept one another with open hearts, full of love and respect, gratitude and sensibility. When we believe in each other and ourselves.

GROWING UP MULTI-CULTURAL

Emigration
The dreams dreamt by longing
The rain cried from longing
The heart is frozen from trembling
In worry sleepless night.

1

Not rubbed shoes of emigration
And not baked cakes for coming back home,
The dust of exclusion
Becomes more and more rankle and oppressive
With each day
And didn't go ways to the infinity
becomes more and more protracted.

Like a dream is a past time.
Which cannot be forgotten?
Like a little-lost child
Wandering in a foreign country.

The doors are locked for coming back,
The roads are closed for coming back.
Eyes wide open, watching,
The heart is asking:' Where is my home?

YOUR FAMILY IS YOUR ROOTS, SOURCE OF YOUR LIFE

I was born in 1970, in Lithuania. Finished Secondary School, attended young philologists, drawing, ceramic and theatre studios while at school. Took part in the creating and establishing the first local TV.

While at school, my poetry was first published in local newspaper, then in national youth magazine.

From my childhood, I was surrounded by books about art and literature. In my parents' house, there were a lot of artworks and fiction literature library. I often visited art exhibitions, museums, art galleries and was reading a lot of different kind of books – legends, myths, fairy tales. And reading poetry especially.

After secondary school, I finished University with a Philology and Ethnology Bachelor's Degree.

In my very young years, I understood the power of words – they can heal, or they can kill. Maybe because my native Lithuanian language is one of the oldest languages in the world. Or maybe because we spoke five different languages in my family. That's mean I was influenced by five different cultures and also from different faiths. I can speak five different languages. From my childhood, I learned how different cultures and traditions could cooperate with each other with respect and understanding or how they can reject each other with no respect and no wish to understand. I felt myself different, growing in multilingual and multicultural family, and I found it very strange that some people could talk and understand just one language and understand things only through the one cultural perspective.

From early on I developed a great interest in the historical development of language, the structure and the meaning of words, As well as Philosophy and Religious Science.

Ethnological studies allowed me to know and understand the secrets of human culture in the ancient world, their understanding and expression of the main things of life – birth, journey in life and death. Myths, legends, fairy tales – it's a code of reasons and consequences, of choices and decisions between life and death.

I was very close to my teachers – at school, at university and in my life. I am grateful to all of them for their support and everything they taught me, especially to one of my first teachers, as well as my parents and my relatives.

BLESSING AND HOPE

"Every Day That Ends, Is a Blessing.
Every Day That Comes, Is Hope"

I got married after University and have a great family, my loved ones – my husband and my son. My husband is also from very a multicultural family. So, our son has had many different cultural influences to his character.

I had a cancer – melanoma - when I was 29 years old, and my son was just 2 years old. After the operation, the doctor told me that he did for me everything he could, and now everything is in God's and my hands. And these words made me think a lot about life and what I could do to make my life better and enjoyable. f. I am not someone who gives up. I can't give up because I have to raise my son; he needs me; and I have to do everything to change my lifestyle and live longer, because of him.

I changed my diet. I started to do yoga, and I spent a lot of time praying, meditation it is like a spiritual cleansing. My biggest wish has been to recover and be alive for a very long time. I have learnt to understand how much life is worth; what love and hope are; how important real support is; what warm words and true actions mean. from all your heart. And how important being together and spent time together is. And how important to believe in yourself is.

It was one of the most important lessons in my life - to understand how short and fragile everything in that life can be, and how short the time we have for our own journey from birth to the death can be. And how irresponsible we are usually wasting our time for things that do not matter. I have also learnt that there is only one most important thing in our life – love, and nothing else. And how a powerful can love to be.

I am grateful to my mum, to my family, to my friends, to my doctors and to all the people who helped me during those difficult time, which led to the greatest changes in my life.

Listen whisper of rain
It tells you a story
About the gates of life
You've just entered,
About the strange time
And strange world,
You're naming
By very strange words:
To be, to live, to love, to continue...
Listen whisper of rain -
It sings you a song
About ancestor's garden,
Where you need to find
A miracle root of your life -
Just then
You'll become yourself
And will be allowed
To continue your journey.
Listen whisper of rain.

WHEN THE CATERPILLAR THOUGHT HIS LIFE WAS OVER, HE BECAME A BUTTERFLY

My experience of Diversity moving to the UK. I came to Peterborough in 2009 to visit my brother during Easter. He told me that I could stay here for as long as I wanted, and he would help me to settle in the beginning.

I just felt that that's the place where I should be. I saw a lot of possibilities to build the life I wanted, and especially possibilities to build a better life for my son. We went back to Lithuania after the Easter holidays, and I told my husband that we had to try new possibilities in another country.

The economic crisis 2008 affected my country badly that many people from my country left to look for a better life elsewhere. My husband and I decided to come to UK for three months, during the summer holiday. We left our son to my Mum during that time, and we came to Peterborough to work for three months. We started working in factories, first in a meat factory, then in a salad and fruit factory. It was a very hard work physically; we worked long hours; and spent more time with people whom I did not have anything in common.

Then, we decided to stay in UK for one or more years. We would consider the social and economic opportunities and the stability for our family here, even if we had to do menial factory jobs.

But I wasn't happy to work in a factory. I thought – I came here not just for work but also to enjoy life. I had to look for other opportunities to live the life I wanted if I wanted to have a better, more comfortable life.

And I started to look after the kind of work that would make me happy. The kind of work that will make me grow, not just earning money. My hard work and efforts brought me success. I turned my challenges into opportunities. And all my dreams have come true.

It is important to think about your real aims and objectives before moving to another country. Start by learning the language and as much as possible about the country you're moving in. It will help you to overcome the challenges you will face.

WHEN YOU STRIVE WITH ALL YOUR HEART; THE WHOLE UNIVERSE HELPS

I was walking one day on one of the main Peterborough streets, and I saw a note at the door of one shop: "Teachers needed at Lithuanian Saturday School." My heart rejoiced – I found what I wanted, job for my heart and on my speciality!

I started working at Peterborough Lithuanian Saturday School "Amber"as a teacher in 2009. I love working with kids, teach them all interesting things and show them directions in their lives.

When I started working at Peterborough Lithuanian Saturday School 'Amber', there were about 10 kids in the School with only two teachers, the Head and Founder of the School Jolanta Kensminiene and me. Because the premises were not adapted for the teaching of the children, the Head and Founder. I went to ask for help from Peterborough City Council h for more space for our the school. .

We were invited at a meeting at the Peterborough City Council by the Community Cohesion and Diversity Team Manager at the time, Mr Jawaid Khan, who is now the Head of Community Resilience and Integration regarding our request. This meeting was a determining factor in my future life in Peterborough. These two people have become more important in my life and my work here. I am very grateful to them for all their help, advice and support. Thanks to that City Council Officer we have received suitable premises for our Saturday School.

We have more than ten classes at our School now and more than ten teachers and up to one hundred kids. We have Lithuanian kids folk dance group, and Lithuanian music group at our Saturday School. I was doing craft, applying an old technique, with different traditional Lithuanian materials, such as clay, yarn, textile, paper, etc. We have our traditional celebrations and events based on our heritage and traditions, our historically important dates. We try to pass on to our children and keep our Lithuanian traditional heritage, Lithuanian language and traditions, to help them understand their identity and remind them about their cultural and ethnic origins.

In 2010, I changed jobs from working in a factory to work at a warehouse. It was hard physically, but a bit better in the working conditions. I had more free time for myself and do other things

Then, the Head Teacher of Peterborough Lithuanian Saturday School, Jolanta Kensminiene, offered me to attend the UK Lithuanian Schools teachers' seminar at the Lithuanian Embassy in London. We went to the seminar together, and it was the beginning of the great enduring and mutual cooperation between us and the Lithuanian Embassy in London. Jolanta and I have become the representatives of Peterborough Lithuanian School at the Lithuanian Embassy in London and in the UK Lithuanian Community.

That cooperation was based on education, cultural, social and other sectors. We also received an invitation to attend the World Lithuanian Communities Schools seminar in the Lithuanian capital, Vilnius, in the summer. I went to that seminar, and it was the start of a mutual cooperation with the World Lithuanian Community, the World Lithuanian Schools, and the Lithuanian Education and Cultural Institutions.

Coming back from our first the UK Lithuanian School seminar in London, we decided that we had to establish a magazine for Lithuanians in Peterborough. We wanted it to be the space for Lithuanians in Peterborough to share ideas, offer and get a professional help and information. We then created the the Lithuanian Magazine, and called it Lighthouse. The first publication came out in December 2010. We were very happy and delighted with the first and nicest feedbacks from our readers. Jolanta took the overall management responsibility of the Magazine, and I became the Editor. My husband Rimantas Grublys was the photographer. He did the, layout and advertisement for the Magazine. Our Lithuanian priest from London, Father Petras Tverijonas helped us with the publishing; a Lithuanian businessman, Aidas Meckauskas, sponsored our Magazine. The Peterborough City Council also sponsored our Magazine later.

I started to conduct interviews with the people who are doing interesting and important things in their lives and other people's lives. I then wrote articles about them and about things that were going on in Peterborough. In the process, I've met a lot of interesting and creative people - businesspeople, artist, sportsman, council officers and so on. I started to build contacts and cooperation between Peterborough Lithuanians and other communities from different background and organisations and institutions.

Jolanta and I, have become official representatives of Peterborough Lithuanians in the Peterborough City Council and other city communities, institutions and organisations.

Step by step with a big help and support of Peterborough City Council Head of Community Resilience and Integration, Mr Jawaid Khan, we have achieved a lot for our people in the city. Our community has become visible, known and respected.

THERE IS NO ONE FELLOW TRAVELLER ON YOUR JOURNEY OF LIFE

Our Magazine "Švyturys" (Lighthouse) was registered as a UK Lithuanian Press, and we started to cooperate much closer with Lithuanian institutions and organisations.

Special thanks to our first Lithuanian, St. B. Vaitkevicius who came to Peterborough in 1948 from Germany refugees camp after the Second World War. We became friends when I went to his house to do an interview about him for our Lithuanian Magazine,

Lighthouse. He has become a patron, a supporter, an adviser, a teacher and a great friend. He introduced me to many people who have also become very good friends with me up till now. Throughout his 50 years of voluntary service as a long-serving member of Peterborough Lithuanian Community, he held important positions in several organisations, including in the Knights of St Columba and the Scout Association. In 2015 Mr Vaitkevicius was awarded the Peterborough Civic Award for his Lifetime Achievements, and in 2017 he was awarded the Order of the Diplomatic Star, a distinction in the Lithuanian Diplomatic Service.

"I am proud that my efforts to give him these awards have been achieved."

St. B. Vaitkevicius invited me to participate at Peterborough Central Library curated project, "Forty Years On "I was asked to share my story of emigration. My story was recorded, and it's kept at Peterborough Central Library archives. It was an interesting experience for me, and I enjoyed being part of that project. It was my first project of diversity.

PROFESSIONAL DEVELOPMENT

Working at Lithuanian Saturday School and for Lithuanian Magazine gave me the opportunity to develop professionally and personally.

While cooperating with local authorities, I was offered the voluntary position, in the Peterborough City Council, as a Lay Member of Peterborough Child Safeguarding Board for East Europeans of Peterborough and Cambridgeshire in 2014.

At the same time, I started my Child Care Level 3 studies and successfully finished them at a local college. It was interesting and important for me to understand how the England Education system works.

After these studies, I got an offer to become a School Governor, as a representative for East Europeans at one of the local Schools of Peterborough. It was a new experience for me, and I was very happy to be in that position, as it has enabled me to gain new knowledge and experience while helping others.

Also, I started to cooperate with the Santa Marta Group Initiative – Preventing Human Trafficking and Modern-Day Slavery Project, working together with the Embassy of the Republic of Lithuania in UK, London, UK Lithuanian Community and Peterborough City Council.

I also wanted to cooperate with local professional artists.

In 2014, I started to work with Peterborough Metal Art Gallery on different projects. First, one of the projects was 100 Journals. 100 people from across the city were challenged to keep a journal over a period of 4 months around the themes of creativity, exploration and reflection.

The next project in 2015, was the Harvest Festival, a cultural celebration of the land. The Festival celebrated the relationship between the city and its rural countryside, connecting people to the land and its associated Harvest rituals, whilst promoting local food and its suppliers. At the heart of the festival was the outdoor meal for 500 people created by international artist Studio Orta.

I also took part in the film, Workers. It was researched and co-produced by Ben Rogaly and Director Jay Gearing as part of the Creative Interruptions project in 2017 – 2018. Ten people from different background from Peterborough spent one day with film Director Jay Gearing, telling him their own stories; how their creativity helped them in the routine of hard and long hours working in fields, factories and warehouses.

Additionally, I was involved in the Planet B project in 2017 – for two weeks, a Green Festival initiative organised in partnership with

Green Backyard and PECT. It is an action-packed programme of events, performances, film screenings workshops, artist's commissions, conference and debates; all focused around sustainability. Pickers, Pluckers and Packers – Poetry tours where people could listen to our local poets Keely Mills, Charley Genever, Judita Gru and Kaiva Kukulite recorded poems. We have also we have read our poems at Question Time Cabaret, organised by London based artist Talia Randall. We also have read our poems at Peterborough Museum Squire's Cafe before the premiere of Generation Zero performance, Lamphouse Theatre.

I have read my poems in One Day with Us event 2018, dedicated to Migrants of UK.

I also participated at Spoken Word Tent on local Millfield Festival 2018, reading my poetry and having a slot together with local Lithuanian folk singer S. Arbocius with a theme "Myths & Symbols of a Viking Past. Stories with symbols that traverse the Baltic Seas and Mirror tales of British Vikings."

In May 2016 with the help of Metal Art Gallery, Lithuanian Bookstore in London and the Lithuanian businessman Aidas Meckauskas and Lithuanian business company Floravita and Peterborough Lithuanian Saturday School Amber, I organized the first Poetry Spring in Peterborough. In 2017, I organized the International Poetry Spring Event. It was not just in Peterborough but also in the Lithuanian Embassy in London, in the Lithuanians Communities in Nottingham and Hull. Local poets and musicians from different backgrounds in Peterborough were involved. This event is growing, expanding and is gaining popularity. The Ambassador of the Republic of Lithuania to the United Kingdom, Mr Renatas Norkus participated in the Poetry Spring event in May 2018 with his singing poetry.

POETRY IS HIGH PILOTAGE OF WORDS, HAUTE COUTURE OF MEANINGS

I have experienced many difficulties as an immigrant. These have had an impact in my life. As such, I felt that it is too hard to keep everything bottled up inside. Then, I started expressing my feelings and thoughts by writing poems. Sometimes, I sent my poetry to my friends in Lithuania. All of them started to ask me when I would publish my poetry book. I then decided to publish them. First of all as a gift to my friends. And the book of my meditative – existential poetry 'At the Gates Of Nonexistence' was published at 2010. Here is one poem for you:

Travelling
From Birth to Death -
This is the journey
Just only for you,
Where you have to find
Yourself,
Hidden in the time,
Called Life.

Where you have
To choose up yourself
With every step,
With every moment
Like a glowing mosaic
Recognising yourself
In the chanting of birds
In the blossoms of trees
In the rustle of rain
In the sounds of the silence.

This is your journey,
You have to go
Through the betrayal
Through the heartburning
Through the despair
Through the words of love
Through the homicidal cognition of truth
That you are the Way, The Truth and the Life, -
This is your destination.

YOUR CULTURE, TRADITIONS AND HERITAGE ARE THE SOURCE AND STRENGTH OF YOUR IDENTITY

I've met a lot of different people from different cultures, learned a lot about their traditions and heritage. All my ethnological knowledge helped me to understand and to accept people from different countries with different traditions and different understanding about life and relations, to respect their differences, to learn from these differences and to find aspects which can unite us.

In April 2018 I started to work at Peterborough Museum as an Outreach Project Officer with Migrants Heritage. Working in that position, I understood how important it is for people from different backgrounds to share their cultures, traditions and heritage, to showcase their identities, to have the possibility to cherish their cultural roots, including their native languages.

In 2018 for the first time the Peterborough different communities' heritages were included in the Peterborough Heritage Festival programme Cultural Treasures Tent was created, and one of my responsibilities was to invite as many people, professionals from different backgrounds to participate in this festival as possible. We had artists and artworks from different backgrounds and workshops at our Cultural Treasure Tent., We had food from different cultures and we had performers from different cultures for the main festival arena and for our Cultural Treasures Tent. People were happy to represent aspects of their cultural traditions and heritage in different way. There were new colours, new tastes, new sounds and new experiences of unusual and interesting things for the residents of Peterborough to try.

Different backgrounds Peterborough based painters' artworks exhibition was organised in the Peterborough Museum's exhibition space. The selection of artworks showcases the diverse range of practices undertaken by local artists. With different influences of culture, heritage and interests each artist has their own identity and unique vision.

Contemporary Peterborough has been curated by Sheena Carman, Vivacity Arts Programme Manager. My responsibility was to invite different backgrounds Peterborough based painters to participate in that exhibition. 30 artists participated with their artworks on that exhibition.

Project Story the City in August 2018 was a real celebration of diversity of the city of Peterborough. It was supported by Peterborough Vivacity, Soulfood Productions and the Caravanserai Collective with support from ISD and Google.org.

The mission was to bring together active Peterborians of different religious (and non-religious) beliefs and from different backgrounds, to share their stories about their identities.

The aim was to build a dynamic, living archive, as well as strengthen relations between neighbours; a rainbow of voices from a city steeped in English tradition, and also rich in cultural and religious diversity.

This project was dedicated to Peterborough 900th year anniversary.

For me participating in that project was a great experience of sharing a common sense of humanity, accepting others difference.

COMMUNITY ENGAGEMENT

Being involved in these kinds of activities has enabled me to start to cooperate with communities from different backgrounds. Since, I have been invited to attend or to be involved in their events and projects. And I have invited community members from different backgrounds, the Mayor of the City of Peterborough, other officials of the Peterborough City Council, to attend or to participate in events, such as Lithuanian Independence Day, Lithuanian Books Day, Lithuanian Anthem Singing Day and other.

Attending other communities' events, I've met wonderful lady, Bernadette Omondi, a leader of the Kenyan Community in Peterborough and a Community Connector, currently working for Peterborough City Council. She helped me overcome many challenges I had to go through, and I am very grateful for all her help and support to me. She was like a bridge between different communities and people from different backgrounds, uniting them in communities' festivals, events and projects.

I then became the Chair of Peterborough Lithuanian Community in 2016. My aim was to bring together Lithuanians in Peterborough and create a strong organization, to create an effective structure of that organization, to provide all sort of professional help to members of our community and to build strong bridges between our community and local authorities, other local communities, institutions and organizations, also between our community and the Embassy of the Republic of Lithuania in UK, London, UK Lithuanian Community, Lithuanian institutions and organizations. My previous contacts and experience were very helpful to achieve all of that.

As a local community, we organised a big event, 'Colours of Lithuania' on the Town Hall, to showcase Lithuanian culture, traditions, heritage, cuisine, history and all other important things of Lithuania. The Mayor of City of Peterborough, members of Peterborough City Council and members of Peterborough diverse local communities, and other honourable guests paid tribute to our event.

In August 2017 I stepped down as Chair from the Peterborough Lithuanian Community. Yet, Lithuanian Saturday School, Lithuanian Catholic Church representative, main Peterborough Lithuanian businessman's, Lithuanian artists and Lithuanian charity company Mum's Union members asked me to establish another Peterborough Lithuanian Community. We named it "Lighthouse", and all these people asked me to become a Chair of that newly established community. I was very happy with a new and very professional team. We organised many events and provided help to Peterborough Lithuanians. We organised a meeting in October 2017 with Mayor of the City of Peterborough in Town Hall and famous Lithuanian professor L. Mazylis, who found a copy of the Lithuanian Independence Act in the German Archives, hidden for one hundred years. It was important, because Lithuania was celebrating its 100 years anniversary of its Independence in 2018. We also worked and cooperated with the UK Lithuanian Community Chair D. Asanaviciute and organised in Peterborough a meeting with the famous Lithuanian writer, and TV presenter A. Tapinas, during which the important emigration challenges faced by Lithuanians were discussed.

I made a presentation about my leadership role as a champion of Peterborough Lithuanians at the UK Lithuanian Community Annual General Meeting in the Embassy of the Republic of Lithuania in UK, London in 2017.

We had a big celebration of 10 years anniversary of our Lithuanian Saturday School Amber.

Lithuanian Charity organization Mum's Union organised Charity Ball to raise money for Lithuanian kids with cancer. It was a very successful event; we raised more than 3 thousand GBP.

We inaugurated an Opening Day of Lithuanian Books Shelve at Peterborough Central Library and organised a Christmas Party and Theatre performance for kids at John Clare Theatre in December.

Lithuanian priest from Roma, Vatican, joined us in the Christmas worship.

We had a big three-day celebration of 100 years anniversary of Lithuanian Independence Day in the Lithuanian Saturday School Amber, in the Lithuanian Catholic Church and in most popular Lithuanian restaurant in Peterborough.

We invited the Ambassador of the Republic of Lithuania to UK, London, Mr R. Norkus to visit the Peterborough Lithuanian Saturday School and to meet Peterborough Lithuanians and local authorities on the occasion of the Restitution of Lithuanian Independence on 11 March 2018.

We organised an Easter Event, based on old Lithuanian Easter traditions. The Lithuanian priest from Roma, Vatican, joined us on that celebration. There is already a 10 years Lithuanian tradition to have Lithuanians all over the world to sing the anthem the same day and at the same time. We organised that event, and honourable guests from different Peterborough communities and the City Council attended.

All these activities and the positions I have occupied have been challenging to me, but I have turned these challenges into opportunities to celebrate with a diverse range of people from other communities.

I love my work because I see in it as a huge opportunity to celebrate culture, traditions, heritage, to celebrate to bring different colours in our lives, which is unique, to **celebrate diversity** and to cross politicians usually artificial made boundaries in general language of humanity – communicating between each other with respect and learning from each other with gratitude.

As I end this chapter, I will leave you with some quotes to keep you motivated to 'celebrate diversity';

1. Listen to your heart – she leads you in the right way
2. Never give up
3. Do your best with all your heart
4. Turn your challenges into opportunities
5. Be grateful for everything
6. Share your experience – your knowledge and abilities – and learn from others. It's never late to learn.
7. All boundaries are in your mind - change your mind to cross the boundaries
8. You are unique; your value is independent of any other opinion about you.
9. Who I am – find the answer and be yourself
10. Your culture, traditions and heritage are the source and strength of your identity

Clara Meirdicks

Born and raised in Nigeria. I left Nigeria for Germany for further studies. I was born to late Mr & Mrs Patrick Uwazie, family of seven, in Uwazie's Compound in Ahiara, Imo State Nigeria.

I am a Nurse/Midwife, Respiratory Care Practitioner (dip.) BSc Health and Social Welfare, MSc Psychology holder, striving for more in the academic world. I worked with Coma/Semi coma patients with Life support machines. Indeed, working with these patients have brought me closer to the realities of life. I am involved in so many activities involving women's empowerment both in the church and outside. I am also a freelance, motivational writer, speaker, Poet, and a blogger. I love writing, I love what I do and am very passionate about it. Writing has helped me to fight some silent wars, ups and downs, and have accompanied me in the darkest moments and days. I believe in using my stories to empower, help others and heal my past.

Area of Expertise: Health

Training/Speaking /Seminar Topics: Health/Matters of Africa.

Other Books by Clara:

Author: (1) The Long Journey to Discovering me (2) The Psychological Ride of Yearning for a Child

Co-author: (1) The Perfect Migrant (2) African Women in Europe

Contact Author:

https://www.linkedin.com/in/clara-meierdierks-606001164/

Phone: 004915231790068

Email: claram.author@gmail.com

Parenthood Diversity

A letter to our special bundle of joy. Love you forever.

By Clara Meierdierks

"Those are facts, but facts, to a child,
are merely words to memorize"
- Maya Angelou

I have chosen to write a letter to my daughter who came into this world in a very special way. When I think of celebrating diversity, I think of the 'Psychological Diversity of parenthood.' The Journey for every woman and every family to parenthood is different.

When like me, you have gone through a long journey to get your bundle of joy, you see life with a different lens and celebrate diversity in a richer unique way, because nothing else is as important than the joy from a long journey.

The details of that journey are in my other books. We had our child through a process called 'In vitro fertilisation' or 'IVF'. It is one of several techniques available to help people with fertility problems have a baby. My struggle to cope with life, support of the diverse amounts of people that were there for me through this journey from friend, family to professionals who made it possible for us to have this child. These people came with diverse knowledge, abilities and background. In the same process the journey of going through judgement, and at times unwelcome comments which made me stronger as a person but could easily bring difficulty to an already complicated situation. It is only through the great diverse individuals that I am here celebrating a great gift from God.

I dedicate this piece to all parents and their children. To every couple struggling to have a child. I pray that everyone should have the chance to experience and write something down for her child or children.

FOR YOU OUR BUNDLE OF JOY.

Take these words they are straight from the heart.

Your Papa was so happy to give you this name.

Your name Shanaya" originated from Indian, means Light, truly you are a light to us.

Your Igbo names Ezinne, meaning good mother, was given after your Nigerian grandma,

Your second Igbo name " Chinagorom " - meaning God has vindicated me -

Your names are so adoring, so lovely, full of meanings.

You made my world,

You gave me a reason to live and fight again and achieved my dreams.

I am living my passion as a writer, and I love God more, All because of you

My Angel.

You are a light, and God will continue to help you to shine,

Don't depart from Him.

You are curious, loving, friendly and always happy,

Give the world a bit of your happiness, your kindness and your ways of always saying

Allelujah Amen...

It is our hope that this will guide you,

Even when we are there.

Take our words, dwell on them, stay close to God

You are just a gold, a bundle of Joy and a light to the world.

May God help your light radiate in the world AMEN.

Dearest Daughter,

"Study nature, love nature, stay close to nature. It will never fail you."

- Frank Lloyd Wright.

When you are ripe enough to read this, you will appreciate our love for you. You will get to realise that the journey that led to your birth was not easy for me especially, that the Lord never departed from us.

I, your mother, left Nigeria in 1998 in search for a better life that will help me realise my dreams and help our family in Nigeria out of poverty. This dream was not without challenges.

I was born in poverty, and I realised early what it means to pray, fight and never give up in a diversified world. I would have quit long ago; If I had, I would not have had you my pretty gold.

When you are reading this know that We love you so much, Papa adores you because you brought smiles and laughter into the family again. Grandma and Grandpa cannot have enough of you; for the space, you occupied in their lives.

A Long Way From Home.

I was born into a family full of love, in Umuofor Nnarambia Ahi-ara Mbaise, in Imo state. Your great-grandfather Grandpa Daniel Uwazie had other brothers, Namely: Chief Onyekwere, Agulanna, Eneremadu, Chima. Your late great-grandma Rebecca was said to be a golden woman, with good heart.

As we were told, they were inseparable and lived in a compound system, married many wives in those days and that is why till today we have this big family which is our pride. Unfortunately, a lot have changed, diminished as new generation crops up.

Nigeria is far away from Germany. A land so rich but poor, blessed but cursed at the same time. A land I love so much but cannot want to live there again, because of corruption, mismanagement and insecurity.

Can you Imagine that I feel lonely most times when I think back on how beautiful and peaceful our land was? A land rich in beauty, culture and heritage, and now nothing again?

The love that existed in the family, the togetherness and the joy to see all kids happy there, even when they don't have as much toys as what you have? I grew up without toys, we were happy, because we had our ways then of filling up our childhood plays.

My father, your Nigerian grandfather, died in Nigerian civil war in 1967/70 and my mum your Nigerian Grandma was left to care for us 7.

Your late grandma, my mother worked so hard as a teacher and gave us all education, morally and religiously for our future. She was a quiet, God-fearing, kind-hearted and loving woman. Very industrious and a disciplinarian.

I tried way home to be useful and pray one day to come oversees so that I can work and assist your Nigerian grandma and my siblings at home. Because, I could not bear my mom most times go hungry just for us to eat, almost went begging for us. These broke my heart, and I vowed so early to make it my way, of course with the help of God.

I qualified as a nurse /midwife, worked in many places in Lagos metropolitan, still could not help with the meagre salary I was paid. In 1996/97 I had to travel with Anti Cyrene, to Germany on medical treatment. She had cancer and died 6 months after we came back from Nigeria. You will get to know your Antis and uncle's from Adanne Cyrene as we called her. There is also your uncle's and Anti from Da Cecilia, Da Jacinta, late also. Uncle De Vin, and Uncle Nick are your grandpa's brothers.

I Knew I Must Take A Step.

After the death of my late Anti Cyrene in 1997, my school friend Bolaji Aina from Ondo state a very good friend helped me to come to Germany.

This journey was not easy for me as I had to borrow money suffer threat of deportations, got into situation that was so hard. I even wanted at some stage to relocate to US. I got my permanent stay, and my German passport after long hassle and pains, To God, be the glory.

The Reason Why You Should Know These.

Things are happening every day, both good and bad. The world changed, and the people changed. Whether am there or not, we sure know you will ask at some stage of your life.

Initial Effort to Practice Nurse Midwife in Germany.

I opted to work as a nurse, what they offered me was a nursing assistant work. It was a battle to accept this status as I knew what I could offer to the society. Always give your best, and no one should limit you except if you allow it. I pray you won't allow it.

I must make it I said

"Success is no accident. It is hard work, perseverance, learning, studying, sacrifice and most of all, love of what you are doing or learning to do.

- Pele.

Meanwhile, I could not help home, and that added to my misery, but, still was determined to have my nursing certificate accepted here. I went to `Arbeitsamt` the ministry of work --- and what a lady there could tell me was that I have work and that they cannot help me (meaning, I should remain as a Nursing Assistant). Gosh! I need to make it, but what about the financial support?

I patched, slept here today, slept there tomorrow, and eventually after several rejections of my applications, 6 months after I received a letter from Etienne Krankenhaus in Neuss to do my 6 months orientation programme and exams (Anerkennungspraktikum).

6 months without pay for me was killing, but I was meant to succeed, and I was just lucky I was assigned a supervisor, a good man, may God bless him, I can't remember his name again, but I can always pray for him.

The period of my orientationally programme was not easy.

As a black, and as one who was not so confident with the German language then. I needed to be better and worked harder than the others who were at the same time doing their programmes but had the advantage of coming from East Europe.

How can you rule out me speaking German with accent when I was not born here, I came here with no knowledge of German and at the age of 27 years old, but some made life so difficult for me, but in the end, I had this little paper that was going to set me on a real German employment market as a registered nurse.

My joy knew no bounds.

THE TRUTH

"Truth has no special time of its own. Its hour is now-always (Author: Albert Schweitzer-

Racism, if not Institutional exists, unfortunately, there are most times no proof, but it exists, and most of us have gone through this and still going through it.

Don't forget, you will be challenged, but I trust my God, your light will prevail. You are not different, all creation are from a source, just that some pigments (white, black, Caucasian and so on), don't mind human being that tends to limit and segregate, we all are one, and with love and forgiveness, hatred will be conquered.

My dear daughter, I am telling you this, to prepare you for a journey in a diversified world. We are in a world that has no mercy for lazy and dishonest people. The world changed and so all need to be close to God, pray for wisdom, knowledge and understanding, for that will lead you to the right people, that will help you do the right things.

MY UNCLE DOCTOR UWAZIE AND WIFE,

They live here in Germany, the wife of my uncle we call her Anti, a German, with very good heart full of love. She had no boundary and loved everyone black or white.

She is loved in the family, and we owe a lot to her, because she has done a lot for the whole family.

LOOKING FOR IDENTITY.

"I can be changed by what happens to me. But I refuse to be reduced by it." - Maya Angelou,

Met this guy at my uncle's place from Mbaise, looked kind at sight. He helped me also during my quest for Immigration, and we thought it was love. But that was the worst relationship ever. His sister made life so unbearable for me, and I did not know why I stayed.

It was with him we began the quest to have a baby. Unfortunately, he had a medical issue which made the doctors resolve to us taking IVF trip. We did this 5-6 times, in Dusseldorf teaching hospital (Reproductive centre), Koln, Essen and eventually we travelled to Spain still nothing, happened. I was all the time heart-broken.

We were all getting impatient, the sister a Reverend sister made life so unbearable for me. Created every situation to make me look worse, at a stage she said I was old and can't give her brother a child.

Funny, she knew her brother had medical issue, but she was definite, and at a stage, the pressure was much, and we separated in March 2012. The painted my name, and said all manner of things to hurt me, despite me losing all investment I made with him to him. I lost my sanity, and suffered depression in their hand, but God rescued me.

I may not have been in the position to control all that went wrong then, but like Maya Angelou wrote," that one can decide not to be reduced by them. Yes, I refused not to be reduced by their definitions of me. God helped me.

"Yes, I made decisions that I regret, and I took them as learning experiences. I am human, not perfect, like anybody else.

- Queen Latifah-

You will make your own way, learn yours in your own way, but never at any stage give yourself, and your dreams up, for no challenge, nobody and circumstances should limit your dreams, except you permit it.

Let God be your reason, for He was always my reason, and He will never let you down.

In the Holy Bible, Proverbs has a lot for you "one Prologue" The sage speaks, avoid bad company,

Listen, my child, to your father's instruction, and do not reject your mother's teachings,

They will be a crown of grace for your head, a circle for your neck, if sinners/ bad companies want to pull you in, move away from them (Proverbs 1:8-11).

FAMILY AND YOUR GOD MOTHERS

Without my family, especially Adanne, Da Ange, your God mothers Vivian and sister Gloria, my almighty God, I would have gone insane, 'For what? 'I was blind to see'.

I refused to complain, I needed God ever, and it was now or never. I knew I must change certain things in my life. It was absolutely wrong " I held onto that relationship that was so broken, cold and crowded, and forgot in fears that another opened door could be possible.

Dear bundle of Joy, I am telling you this not to scare you away from the world, just to prepare and encourage you to be careful, and to help you prepare for this busy world. You need God at everything you do and at every step you make.

SIX MONTHS AFTER SEPARATION

I met your dad at one of my shopping at a supermarket, and that was my love, my rescue, my God-sent and we were married, life was for me as I dreamt and hoped. God restored all my past glory, gave me a home, a place of peace and " All worketh for those who believe in God ' I love God, and Please don't fail to seek the face of God anytime, anywhere.

OUR JOURNEY FOR YOU.

We were so much in love. I love your father so much; he is kindhearted and a God fearing and hardworking husband, father and son. He is someone anyone should be proud of, and I am so proud of him and thank God for His gift.

Your dad had a troubled past from his previous marriage, which nearly ruined him. Thank God we were destined from God to meet.

Your dad knew I had so much love for children and did not hesitate to support me in a journey that was to multiply and increase our happiness.

I realised this quote from Thomas A. Edison that says: "Our greatest weakness lies in giving up. The most certain way to succeed is always to try just one more time."

I was ready to try just one more time in this journey.

ONCE CONFIRMED

What is perfect time for you and me?

You will hear sometime, things like; *"wait for a perfect time."* I did not dispute this perfect time, but I thought you can't always wait for the perfect time, sometimes you have to dare to do it because life is too short to wonder what could have been,- Sayingimages.com With the help of some inspirational quotes, reading the Bible, I realise I had to seek for God to help me realise this perfect dream of mine, because I trust that He has a perfect plan for me and that is YOU, my bundle of joy.

"Just because it hasn't happened YET doesn't mean it won't."

- Lifecoachcharlie.com

The whole pains and agony disappeared, I became alive and happy again. Things started having meaning again, because of YOU my bundle of joy.

Once you were handed over to your dad by the doctor, I could not forget the first eye contact, the joy and the tears that rolled down my eyes.

How can I thank God, my family and your God mothers?

You were born in Lagos, that was how we planned it because of your Nigerian Grandmother. She was frail, and we knew that would have given her a reason to smile and live again. Unfortunately, she died six months to your birth; I was so heartbroken, I cried a lot because I needed her to see you, to give you a name and love you like she did to us.

We had to name you after her " Ezinne", good mother.

OUR HUSSLE

"People talk about perfect timing, but I think everything is perfect in its moment, you just want to capture",

-Eddie Huang-

After the normal process which took us nearly two weeks in Lagos to complete your travel documents,

Your Cousin (De Gi Chimeka), was immensely helpful to us, all the runaround, everything was handled, carefully by him.

He is not only your cousin; he will serve the role of a big uncle for you.

All worked out very perfectly in the end for us.

19.08.2016

I was so happy when we got your travelling document and had to confirm our ticket immediately.

We left Lagos that night through Amsterdam, on a KLM airline flight.

For some reason, you cried so much at Muritala International Airport Lagos as if you did not want to come to Germany. We tried everything, and you could not stop crying even in the airplane. The stewardesses gave all sorts of assistance.

Five hours in the air you slept off, and subsequently, you suddenly stopped crying, and everything became normal again, and I was so happy.

MY FIRST CONFUSION.

Though a long journey, a long wait and a beautiful ending. Glory to God.

I have delivered so many women, during the days I worked as a midwife, had had a lot to do with babies, but it is not same as when you are having your own first real experience, at not a very young age, at 47 years of age.

I became so unsure of myself; my husband came to my aid.

We did things together, he supported and encouraged me and helped where he could,

The rest of the journey was so smooth, and eventually, we landed in Bremen, Germany.

20.08.2016.

When the plane touched down at Bremen International Airport, I knew it was going to be another level of challenge, this time very positive one.

My parents-In-law waited with all expectations. We took a taxi from the Airport home, and as we were stepping into the compound, my parents-in-law had decorated all with the words;

"WELCOME HOME BUNDLE OF JOY, WE LOVE YOU"

This touched me and moved me to tears of joy. They took you held you in arm and shed tears of joy.

We were all happy, and You brought us a lot of joy and light.

Your grandparents had organised for all we needed for you, up to baby bath tub, everything: You did not lack anything and life is so beautiful with you.

> *"Parenting is the biggest sacrifice one*
> *can make; It's putting your life on hold*
> *to fulfil the promise of your children's*
> *tomorrow."*
> *- Federica Ehimen*

YOU ARE MY GOLD

Wonderfully made by God,
My beloved child!
I adore you,
Those your childlike acts,
Your baby looks,
ravish me,
My daughter,
My God's gift,
My blessing,
My love,

My bundle of Joy,
You are a blessing enclosed.

You are an ivory,
Your eyes mesmerising,
Your hair the mixture of coil and African like,
How great is our Lord?
To give me a beautiful daughter like you,
I will lead you as the Lord directs,
I will pray for wisdom and greatness in you,
You will be God's apple,
You will Love God, and He will love you
And protect you.
Praise God my Family, My friends.

POEM TWO

When I sleep
I hear your babylike moves,
My beloved,
I leap for joy
As my heart race,
At a little sound from your room,
I get up!
I peep through the holes,
to see you
Sleep soundly,
Be at peace
You belong to me,
My bundle of joy,
My God's gift.
The days of agony were

Filled up the minute
You came,
For your love saved me,
The presence of You,
Cannot be measured,
I long to hold you always,
Never to let you go,
My apple,
My love,
My jewellery,
I love you and cherish you
So much,

My greatest gift.

God used you to wipe tears away
From me,
You are my Gold
And I cherish you.
Know always that
You are my purest gold,
I cannot exchange you for anything,
You are my joy
My heart rejoices,

How nice it is to love you!
To have you in my hand,
To behold you,
And wrap you around me when am home,
I love the mimic you make when am going
Out,
Your baby like protest,

Your cry!

Mama needs to go out sometimes,
Without you,
But you always know that I have you
At heart wherever I go,
That soothes me,
Gives me the greatest Joy.
Tells me you love me,
Reveals to me that "Mama is also gold."

When I am home,
You hear my voice and you
Swing your legs in jubilation,

I see how you struggle to come to Mama,
leaping and swinging,
wanting to free the hold on you.

Screaming loud to let the hand on you go,
For you to jump and hold Mama,
And whisper in your language,
To mama, please Mama,
Never leave me.

I see this and want to cry,
The cry of a sweet Mama,
Whose love is appreciated.

If you grow up,
And read this,
You know Mama is the happiest

POEM THREE

How beautiful you are my daughter,
My love is for you,
Papas pride,
And Mamas bundle of joy,
You make me happy,

You are my rose,
You will bloom and shine,
Your scent will be an aura,
That soothes,

You will be wise,
You will be humble,
You will fear God,

My beloved,
My lovely daughter,

WATCHING YOUR DEVELOPMENT.

"Cherish each moment with your children for you can never bring back their childhood."

- Unknown quotes -

Watching you grown every day, gave me joy and increased my strength, to do more and thank God.

Step by step, you will lose somethings and gain some things that God deem necessary for you.

LOVING YOU

Just touching you every minute, seeing your smiles, your smallest behaviour, leaps my heart.

Goes the saying from Nihil Saluja;

"Being a mother means that your heart is no longer yours; It wonders wherever your children go."

One to five months, you knew immediately and blended in the family. Once you were laid in your bed, you murmured a bit and played in your world and the next minute you were sleeping. Some nights I wake up to check you because we never had any late nights.

So, blessed we were to have you my Gold.

Once you have eaten, you never wake up for anything until the next day, you could in-between make a little noise, or scream for a short while, when we assumed you had a dream, these were just for a second.

I have counted my blessings and thanked God for the gift of you.

You are just one in a million, and I love you more every day.

I heard parents talk about having sleepless nights, but we are blessed. As if you knew mama would need to go to work sometimes.

Having you is just God's perfect gift to me. I can't thank God enough.

YOUR BAPTISM AND BEYOND

At six months you were so active, you loved all that were given to you. Very active. You have lavished attention, very curious in your way. I'm grateful to God. Seven months you were turning very freely, enjoyed. Your walker, started crawling, and saying words like "Dada", laughed, notices Mama, Papa, Omi, Opi. Books and colours attracted you so much.

At eight months so much happened of which we are ever thankful to God. You showed a big concern when other kids around you were crying, your empathy for other kids this is also called "reflexive crying."

Finger foods were good for you. At nine months you improved a lot, babbled with meanings, exhibited sense of humour, said bye, bye at 10 months you were already almost climbing, all you need do is have a hold on something and that was it. I had so much fear.

New faces did not scare you, you insisted on what you wanted.

TWELVE MONTHS

Whoa! what a great God. Your birthday was celebrated in the church and at the church hall, where we organised a great party to thank God and celebrate your one year with other children. 21 was on a Friday, we then agreed to do it on a Saturday On 22 July 2017 at Pfarrhaus Guter Hirt, Lilienthal, and on Sunday we did a small thanksgiving

You know what?

You made all efforts could stand on your own. I prayed you work on your birthday. Somehow, you refused to stand alone on your birthday, but all went well.

We finished around 18 hours that day, cleaned everywhere handed over the key to the hall, and on getting home, my Gold refused to be carried and made her first bold step.

And from that time, she made her bold step; nothing could ever stop her again.

THE REST OF THE MONTHS
TILL YOU TURNED TWO YEARS OLD.

Were months of exploration. Took active part in (Kindergruppe), crash. We allowed you to set the pace, no rush. You did not want to use your walker. A lot improved

You showed your willingness to help at home, tried to imitate everyone and everything we do.

We are so proud of you. Thank God you are seldomly ill. Only twice during this time that you had fever that lasted for 2 days. We never noticed when you were growing teeth.

My God is amazing" When God works, He perfects all.

Today as I am rounding up my chapter in 'Celebrating Diversity' book, this piece is for you, you are two and how else can I thank God.

Who chose a perfect time,

To give us a perfect child,

With a beautiful home,

Loving father, husband, Opi and Omi.

We are blessed.

One-year Birthday.

First Inquiry on Nursery 03/05/18: Mummy and daddy were excited to make this move for you.

Two Years.

"Success is built upon pillars that shake but don't fall. Move on boats that brave the oceans currents but don't capsize and fly on the wings of mighty birds that fly on no matter where the destination be."

- Hermann J Steinherr

My dear daughter, learn well. There is a good God who cares for all you are and do,

Always do good,

"For the day comprises of adequate moments for us to do a little good for someone every day of our lives."

- Hermann J Stenherr

"Love yourself. It is important to stay positive because beauty comes from the inside out."

-Jenn Proske -

Above all... with love, you can change a lot.

Love is the only one thing that the world is lacking today, the only honest and priceless thing that we need to conquer hatred, discriminations and indifferences. The only thing that knows no difference in religion, culture, colour and sex, and reaching others as well as reaching dreams together.

"In other to help others, to serve others, the real motive is love." - Dalai Lama.

The desire to reach for the stars is ambitious; the desire to reach hearts is wise ",- Rick Sutter -

So, daughter, be wise, Love God because He loves you, be kind to people, be honest and be careful, be courageous and learn to speak out boldly and with respect. Listen, interpret, pray for wisdom, be patient, generous and kind, be happy, you can't always win, be ready for some failures, challenges, and be ready to try over and over, and over again until you succeed. Try everything, learn all you can, you can always succeed, for as Maya Angelou cited in - Letter to my daughter- *"Since one person, with God, constitutes the majority." Let wisdom guide you.*

WISDOM

A strong tool
Use it
Knowledge will take over,
When prudence is at guard,
And lead you away from ungodly and dangers,
Keep you off roads with stings,

TO OTHERS READING THIS:

"Through a long and painful process, I´ve learned that happiness is an inside job- not based on anything or anyone in the outer material world. I've become a different and better person- not perfect, but still a work in progress."

- Alan Stewart.

I dedicate this piece to all parents and their children. To every couple struggling to have a child. I pray that everyone should have the chance to experience and write something down for her child or children.

I have had ups, downs, failed many times, had successes too and am grateful to God. All that happens in our lives are most times, not our ends. Everything that happens is a process. Nothing comes easy, life is complex, and we make mistakes in our journeys.

We should not let our mistakes be a reason why we stopped developing our future and aiming at our dreams.

Children are gifts from God and should be handled with love and care. They are the future of a nation, the pillar and the hope of our tomorrows, so *"Handle with care."*

Let them know they are important and loved, give them love and you will get that in return.

Teach them good behaviour from home. Teach them to smile from their parents.

"Spend quality time with your children to make them feel loved, wanted, worthy and build their self-esteem up, so they go out into the world with confidence. "

- Nishan Penwar.

I thought of what to leave behind for my daughter, even when we are there. All I could think of doing is to help her through this piece to adjust to a world and let her see all as equal, love and respect others irrespective of their background, while at the same time being careful, wise and close to God.

I pray to God to give us the longevity, good health to see you grow into that promising lady God created you to be.

I can't tell you how long it took me to put all these down but am sure, and I hope those reading this will see meanings in this piece.

Every child is "Goldwert" (worth gold), they need to know their worth, even when we are there.

They need to be encouraged to believe in themselves, because we are in a very competitive world that has no mercy, let them know "

"Nobody can make them feel inferior without their consent. Let them know They should have dreams for themselves and work hard to make those dreams come true. If hard work is not enough, they should then fight for it."

- Eleanor Roosevelt.

The world is the way it is because we all have become so careless, lost touch with God, speaks and spread hates instead of love. Go about with unforgiving hearts and pass on to our children.

We should not forget to tell our children that the greatest healing therapy is friendship and love.

The world is our collective responsibility, and we have the collective responsibility to care for our world. Let us start right now;

to say the right things to our children,

to live a life, not just a life, a life full of meaning, full of love, forgiving hearts, a brother or sister's keeper.

"Let the beauty of what we love be what we do." -Rumi.

Let us all make the world a better place for us to live, raise and love our children. Let us all today, change something, if it is not working, to help us live a written legacy to the present and on-coming generation. For

"A tree is known by its fruit; a man by his good deeds. A good deed is never lost; he who sows courtesy reaps friendship, and he who plants kindness gathers love."

- Saint Basil

Mother Teresa once said, let us always meet each other with smile, for the smile is the beginning of love. Let us be a good teacher that can inspire the imagination and instil a love of learning.

Our bundle of joy we love you unconditionally, and pray you grow in God's way, and be what God wants you to be.

If you take our words, and turn your ears to the words of God, you will realise how easy it could be in a busy world of today, and how everyone can help make the world safe for diversified ideas, culture, religion and beliefs.

You will control technology and technology will not control you Amen.

"Always pay attention to our words, to you we will pour our hearts."

- Proverbs 1:23

You are blessed forever Amen.

Thank you all for sparing your time to read my chapter. God bless you.

"There is beauty in difference. No one is born a racist! Teach love and respect and welcome diversity."
- Sarah Moores.

Ali Abdoul

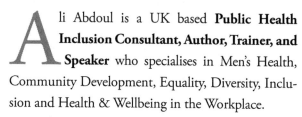

Ali Abdoul is a UK based **Public Health Inclusion Consultant, Author, Trainer, and Speaker** who specialises in Men's Health, Community Development, Equality, Diversity, Inclusion and Health & Wellbeing in the Workplace.

He has more than 20 years' experience helping policy makers, mainstream leaders, and communities to collaborate and promote community cohesion, health and well-being through inclusion, advocacy, and educational programmes, using multi-disciplinary approaches.

He has two daughters and two older stepdaughters and enjoys reading and researching.

Training/Speaking /Seminar Topics: (1) Public Health Inclusion: Men's Health, (2) Equality and Diversity, (3) Community Development, Health & Wellbeing in the Workplace.

Books written or co-authored including current book:

Celebrating Diversity: Positive Stories of Migration from Around the World.

BLACK MEN IN DENIAL? Challenging Social Beliefs on Black Men and Prostate Cancer

Company/Business Name: Diverse Cultures Ltd

Contact Details:

LinkedIn: https://www.linkedin.com/in/ali-abdoul

Facebook: https://www.facebook.com/ali.aw.abdoul

Twitter: https://twitter.com/AliAbdoul8

Instagram: https://www.instagram.com/aliabdoul6/

Phone: +44 (0) 7397010685

Email: Ali@diverse-cultures.co.uk | ali.abdoul1166@gmail.com

Websites: www.aliabdoul.com |

Diversity: Is it Black or White?

By Ali Abdoul

"The lessons I learned as a professional on the field of Equality and Diversity before the inclusion buzz."

I am writing this to share my journey and my take on diversity and inclusion from growing up in one of the least diverse countries in the world, to living in some of the most diverse places and spending many years working in the field.

I was born in Madagascar by migrant parents from the Comoro Islands or Comoros. When I was five, my mum decided that she wanted to go back home, and obviously she took my two brothers and me with her. I grew up and had my school education in Comoro.

The Comoro Islands is a small country situated in the Indian Ocean between Madagascar and the African mainland.

It is a Muslim majority country with a mixture of African, Arab, Persian, French and other influences. Each one of these cultures stands out in different ways. However, the most dominant cultures are the African and Arab cultures. Which means you may find some people who have clear complexion and others with very dark complexion and those in between. Already you can see the diversity of origins which blended to result into specific Comorian identity today. I identify myself as a being a Muslim, French in my official papers and Black African.

Today, I can celebrate all this heritage strongly with pride. People in the Comoros today strongly believe that our roots are middle eastern but also African. The official language in the country today is French and Arabic.

I am educated into the French schooling system, from primary school all the way up to secondary school. Obviously as a Muslim those days, the first school you go was Qur'anic school before going to French school. It was the norm when I was growing up in the 1970s and 1980s.

I am married and have children. Two younger ones, Naila and Iman and I have two grown-up stepdaughters, Ngweshe and Ngosa.

MY JOURNEY TO EUROPE

After graduating from secondary school in 1988, I taught for one year in year 1 to year 4 in secondary school. Because of the shortage of teachers, it was very common that immediately after graduating from secondary school you teach for a minimum a year before going to higher education. It was considered as some sort of national service.

It was the norm that those who graduate from secondary school are in most cases helped by their families to go to study abroad. Those who can afford would go further afield to France, Morocco, Senegal and other African French-speaking countries.

Others would settle for Madagascar. It was close to the Comoro Islands and did not cost a lot more than it did in France or Morocco or Senegal. In sum, people tend to go where they got a place.

There was a national College that, at that time could only train journalists and teachers. It was small to the point that not everybody graduated from secondary school had a place. Only few privileged ones.

I always thought that I would go to university to continue my education. However, I did not have any idea what a university was like. I only wanted to go as far I could go. It was a young boy dream.

You see, I loved going to school. Not only did I love going to school, but I also believe school saved me. It was one of those places where I felt the most comfortable. I felt happy when I was at school to the point that I got very sad when, for whatever reasons, the teacher or one of the teachers was absent. I could not even understand why most of my classmates would be jubilant at the idea of not having class.

I enjoyed being out with my friends as well, playing football and other kind of sports and games or going to the beach and so on. Believe or nor not, I enjoyed being out very much to the point my mum would always come out searching for me to go and eat.

Anyway, when I graduated from secondary school, I was eager and looked forward to pursuing my studies at university. At that time, I had just happened to have my French passport done. So, it seemed natural for me to go to France. It was also the opportunity to meet my father whom I had never met, with no expectation. Just wanted to meet him.

I then moved to France in 1989 and enrolled in Philosophy at the Universite de Provence, Aix-En-Provence. However, before I could finish my degree, I was conscripted into the French army. In France, until the mid-1990s, every male aged 18 had to spend at least a year in the army. I tried to postpone the conscription until I completed my degree, but the army refused. So, I had to cut short my studies and go to the army; otherwise, I could have ended up in jail.

Although I did enjoy university and my time in the army, I had never felt settled in France. Something I never managed to explain. I only felt it. I had many friends and many relatives; I knew the history, the culture and the language.

After a year in the army, I went back to university. This time, I enrolled in English. I started learning more about British culture, literature, the language and so on. When I was in my second year. I decided to go to United Kingdom to enhance my English. I had planned to stay for 10 months and go back to France to continue my studies. However, I enjoyed my stay in Edinburgh so much that I decided to stay in the UK, which I did. That was back in 1996, and I have been living in the UK since then.

It was my love of the English language and the UK that brought me to the UK. This started when I was in my last year in primary school. When I was preparing for the entrance exam to secondary school, I would spend time, during the weekend, revising with some classmates in the village schools. Those who were in secondary school would also come to use the school.

One day I was passing by one of the schools, then I heard this interesting sound. It was neither French nor Arabic nor the local dialect. I was mesmerised by it, and I stopped and continued listening. That was the first time I heard English. I loved it immediately. For some reasons, I found it beautiful and interesting. The first thing I learnt was to count from 1 to 10. I was so excited that I could that. At that time, English was only taught in secondary school. While in secondary school English became one of my favourite subjects.

Son once in France, studying English at university; my knowledge about the English language, the British culture and civilisation increased. This gave me extra motivation to want to go to the UK.

Initially, as I mentioned earlier, I didn't plan to stay in the UK. It was just a few months trip to go and get familiar with the language particularly the spoken language and go back to France and finish my studies. But then I came, and I fell in love with the country and I never went back to France.

THE DIFFERENCE BETWEEN MIGRATION AND DIVERSITY

There is a difference between migration and diversity. I understand migration as the movement of people and sometimes even animals from one place to another. This can be an internal migration as well as external. In this case, from one country to another.

As for diversity, I see it as being the differences in characteristics of the people moving from one country to another. Such characteristics could include nationality, race, ethnicity, gender, sexual orientation, socio-economic status, age, cultures, physical abilities, religion or beliefs, political beliefs, educational background, marital status, and so on.

Moreover, diversity incorporates the notions of acceptance and respect. This means understanding and recognising that each one of us is different and uniqueness, because we have different characteristics. This also means that, despite our differences, we all deserve to be treated with respect and dignity, regardless of our characteristics. without discrimination because

Embracing and celebrating diversity is about creating and fostering a safe, positive and nurturing environment that enables each one of us to access opportunities, grow and be successful regardless of our individual characteristics. An environment where individuals or groups can go on enjoying life free from prejudice, where equality, social justice and mutual respect are inherent to us.

Furthermore, embracing and celebrating diversity also includes how to relate to those characteristics or to the people with characteristics that are different from ours, and the recognition that no culture is inherently superior to another

Looking back diversity is not something that people talked much about. I only grew up noticing I am different from others, not knowing exactly what it meant.

It was when I came to Edinburgh and started working in the equality field that I started realising what it means to be different and how this relates to people, places, aspirations, happiness, opportunities and so on. And that diversity is not something we need to learn; it is inherent to us. We were born with differences characteristics and grew up recognising them in others.

I have come to realise that diversity has always existed and wherever I go in the world those differences exist.

However, when I arrived in Edinburgh, I did not have such insight, at least consciously. Like any other migrant in a foreign land, it was difficult at the beginning. Not knowing what was going on, the local customs and etiquettes; I was a bit nervous. I did have any idea what to expect.

I said to myself; I love the English language, and I am in an English speaking, "go out there and practice". It was the best opportunity for me mainly, when I decided to go back to university.

I lived far from the city centre and whenever I had the time I took the bus to the city centre not knowing what to expect. I went to museums, libraries and tourist information centres. I would follow the tourist trail to make sure I learnt as much about Edinburgh and the whole UK as possible. I would go out on my own to nightclubs, pubs, cinemas, theatres and so on.

As I was getting familiar to the place, I started understanding and learning the way of life in the city. Confidence started growing and I no longer worried about people's reactions. Which helped me a lot to settle quickly at university.

I found the people very nice and welcoming. They contributed to making my experience very enriching. Although I didn't know what to expect, I think it was a good thing that my UK experience started from Edinburgh.

I lived in Edinburgh for 10 years and visited many places in Scotland. During that time, I had never come across harsh racism. There were those occasional moments where a drunken person would look at me and say, "go home what are you doing here?". I heard that a lot.

Interestingly, at the beginning, even if I was racially discriminated, I wouldn't know. It was later that I started realising that I experienced racism several times.

This brought me back to the time I spent in the French army. I remember one day a guy called Etienne approached me and started feeling my hair, saying things like, "this might be a big shock for you, coming from the African jungle to a big place like this. Can you sleep in a bed? Obviously not, this is not like you hut in Africa". He even asked me if we had schools, if I ever wore clothes and shoes before I came to France.

I was surprised and sad to find out later that Etienne was one of those young people classified as not in education, employment or training (NEET). He could not properly read or write. At that time, we didn't have internet or smartphone. Because, we were far from home and sometimes it could take months before being allowed to go home for a weekend, the most affordable way to get in touch with friends and family was to write. He was not the only, though. I used to help them write letters to their friends. I would even read the letters they received. Etienne and I became friends. He even apologised to me for the way he behaved towards me. He realised that, although true I came from Africa, I was not ignorant. I was educated and knew more about the French culture, history, civilisation and language than he previously thought.

I also remember another situation in the hotel I used to work. One day, while at work, I went to the toilets and I found this inscription on the wall. It read, "you bloody foreigners go home". What was bizarre about the message what was used to write it. It appeared to me like whoever wrote it, used their stool to write it. I was then thinking that this person might have a lot of hate to do that. Although it was not directed at me personally, as a foreigner, I felt that I was included. It was my first experience of racism in the UK. I went I talk to one of the senior managers. I was hoping that he was going to do something to get to the bottom of the situation, even though I had no idea, what he could do at that time.

Interestingly the following day when I came back to work I found the toilets closed without any explanation. There was a note saying, "please do not use these toilets.

I don't think many people knew what really happened in the closed toilets. It took about a month before the toilets were open for use. I tried once to ask the manager if he knew the culprit. He never answered, and I gave up.

Another situation I only understood later that I was discriminated. I believe that I was passed over for promotion several times while working in the same hotel as above. You see, the people who were appointed managers while still working in the hotel went to the university like me. In fact, I started working there before them. I even trained them when they started. I enjoyed the job and won many praises from customers and managers alike.

I was so good and well experienced to the point that no VIP would be looked after by anybody else other than me. Even, there were time times when I was called while I was off because the head of the whole company was coming to the hotel and the manager was not confident enough to leave him and his guests to the care of other members of staff.

Yet, whenever there was an opportunity for promotion, I never knew about it. This happened several times. I then decided that I needed to live if I wanted to progress. I was even put off by the hotel industry in general because of the attitude of the hotel towards my career progression.

I remember the day I told my colleagues and managers and some regular customers that I was leaving. Many were sad that I was leaving. The following day the managing director called me into his office and tried to convince me to stay. But I had already made up my mind. I said no despite his insistence. My enthusiasm had diminished; I was no longer enjoying working in the hotel.

I have learnt a lot since 1996. I realised that diversity is not about black and white issue. It has been with us forever. Each one of us is different and unique. Even if we come from the same family, the same culture or the same race or the same belief; we have characteristics that are visible and invisible that are different from others.

Unfortunately, some people will discriminate against you because of these characteristics. Sometimes, such discrimination starts from home. Unknowingly, I would think that was just normal and confidently ignore and move on. Or you know push you back or whatever.

Looking back and knowing what I know now I can ascertain that I experienced discrimination on several occasions since I was young.

But I remember when I was in secondary school, I saw many classmates being abused and belittled by other city dwellers classmates because they came from the countryside. The city dwellers classmates believed that were civilised and superiors to those coming from the countryside. Sometimes, they behaved as if the school belonged to them, and that they could do whatever they want without them being disciplined. The attitude was that people from the countryside were savages, uncivilised and that their place in the farm not at school. Although, many classmates would ignore such abuse, I am sure some were affected. Some schoolmates might have stopped going to school because of such experience.

I grew up believing each one of us deserves every respect. I think that that where my passion for fighting against prejudice and promoting equality and social justice came from.

My faith also taught me that everyone needs to be treated well with dignity and respect. Behaving arrogantly towards others is against my faith.

It is important to note that because people are from the same culture, the same ethnicity and so on, doesn't necessarily mean that they do not discriminate against each other. Those who want to discriminate always try to find justification for doing so.

LIFE BACK IN COMOROS AND SUBTLE CLASS SYSTEMS

Class is also another issue. Some people believe that they are from the upper class. What they understand by that is that they think they can ill-treat other people; say and do whatever they want, and nobody should react to their behaviour. They have the right and that's it.

Although, this is not a formal or official thing, a class system does exist in the Comoro Islands. Obviously, from the outside, it is not visible. You have to understand the cultures, the customs and traditions to be able to notice that. It is not because we are bound by these traditions or faith, that people get along. In some situations, people from other town would not marry someone from another or village.

People sometimes just grow in confidence and deal with things you know or push those things back and not let these affect them.

I believe when people learn to know you; they would understand how hurtful their behaviour and attitudes are to others.

Unfortunately, it is part of human nature. Even in the family, you would find such discrimination because of your characteristics or situation.

I lost my mum when I was very young and had never seen my father. I was an orphan by the age of eight or nine. I remember instances where I was treated ill-treated because I did not have a mum and dad. Some people would even make jokes about my dad who they had never met. That was the first time I came across such justification for abusing someone. I never told anybody, but I was really hurt. However, I was strong mentally and spiritually. It was easy to move on.

I knew that from a very younger age that from now on people would look at me differently because of being orphan. So, therefore, from that moment I was put in a different class in the family. These things can affect people.

THREE LESSONS FOR THE READER

Three things I would like to share with you dear reader are:

1. It doesn't matter where you are in the world; you will notice diversity. People are different in their characteristics; some try to use these differences as justification to abuse others. The fact that people are bound by the same culture, race, religion or belief doesn't necessarily mean they get along.

2. In terms of people celebrating the diversity of what we have. Generally, we are predisposed to look at people differently depending on their circumstances and characteristics. Again, that doesn't matter where you are in the world, whether in a small country like the Comoros or you are in a bigger country like the UK or France. You

know people are people, and there will be different. And it's just how you connect with those differences.

3. What I can advise is how you deal with things. It is not about how people treat you because people treat you how they want regardless of where you are, who or what you are. But it's your own personal response that would determine how you move forward in the situations that you're faced with.

Obviously, we all deal with situations differently but sometimes you focus on what is more important and helpful to you, and not let the negatives affect you. You know that wherever you go, you might find yourself in some situations where some people try to show off or put you down, because they arrogantly believe that they're better than you.

Uk Life and Professional Career.

I had just completed my degree in Hospitality and Tourism Management and decided to settle in the UK. It was not part of the initial plan. It just happened. When I enrolled in the course, my thoughts were that once I finished, I would go back to the Comoros Islands.

I then I changed career and industry completely. I joined the community, and voluntary sector where I felt would make a big difference in people lives. Equality, diversity, social justice, community cohesion and inclusion were some of the motivators.

I started learning new things, discrimination in the UK, anti-discrimination law, equal opportunity, community development, government policy to tackle racial discrimination, and many other things. I started helping people experiencing discrimination, working with and advising local governments and other local players on issues related to racial discrimination, diversity and community cohesion.

For over 20 years I have seen many changes in this country, in terms of how migrants were treated then and are now and what the government have done to reduce discrimination and prejudice towards migrants.

I lived in Edinburgh, Scotland for 10 years. I was partly educated there and had travelled almost everywhere in the country. I love Scotland. I had many friends and felt comfortable and welcomed by the local people. The landscape was also attractive.

Despite that, racial discrimination was still an issue. We had to work hard to bring people together with local authorities, civil society organisations and groups, and communities to educate people on the issues of racism and its devastating effects on people, diversity and community cohesion and most. It was also important to provide support to victims of racial discrimination, empower them to be who they were with confident and so on.

We ensured that local practices reflect national anti-discrimination laws. We worked to make sure that black and minority communities were not ostracised and marginalised but empowered to get involved and had a voice in local decision making.

We worked to eliminate racial discrimination, promote equal opportunity for all and ensure that people were not discriminated because of their race colour, ethnicity or national origin and could access education, employment, housing and other life opportunities like every other section of the society.

I also learnt a lot in the process about local culture, etiquette, customs and traditions. One of the things I did when I first arrived in Edinburgh was to get out and learn as much as possible about local people, their ways of life and so on. I went to places where I found myself being the only black, with all eyes looking at me as if they were saying, "what are you doing here? you are at the wrong place."

I don't drink. One day I walked into one of the very popular pubs in Edinburgh. I walked to the counter and ordered a glass of coca cola. I could feel the eyes of the people on me, as if I had just said the most ridiculous thing nobody ever heard. Confidently with a bit of naivety, I took my pint of coca cola and moved on, without paying much attention to eyes following me.

I would walk into pubs and enjoy the local and traditional cuisine, meeting the people and learn about life in general.

It was a very good experience. It can be scary at times, being new in a foreign land. But it can also be rewarding when you get out there and learn as much as you can about local culture.

With this kind of attitude, I found myself in the forefront of a lot of changes in the equality and diversity arena. At that time, I would say, the focus was about eliminating racial discrimination and promoting equal opportunity. It was about fostering an environment where people have equal chance in accessing education, employment, housing and services. Recognising and celebrating diversity was something that came years later.

My area of work involved promoting equal opportunities and advocating for the issues affecting people from black and minority ethnic communities. This involved working with local communities, local authorities, the police, the National Health Service, schools and so on. My work also involved about educating and empowering communities and bringing communities together to ensure we were in the best position to scrutinise and advise local authorities on racial discrimination matters and that anti-discrimination laws are understood and applied as intended.

I remember back in when the Race Relations (Amendment) Act 2000. It was a breakthrough in anti-discrimination laws and policies. It imposed duties on local authorities to eliminate racial discrimination and promote equal opportunity and good race relations between people of different race.

This came into existence just after the Stephen Laurence Inquiry which reported that institutional racism existed within the police.

The years that followed gave communities confidence. At last, we were not bumping onto steel walls anymore. This time local authorities had to work with us because of the legal obligation imposed on them. Before, the amendment they didn't have to. This obviously helped things forward.

Diversity became something to be recognised, embraced and celebrated. It was about opening doors for people regardless their cultural background. It was about reminding each other that we were all different and none of us should feel about it. Diversity is good, and there is nothing to fear about it.

WHERE THE EQUALITY WORK STARTED

I was involved with the African Centre Scotland. It existed to promote equal opportunities for people of African origin who lived in Scotland, fight against racial discrimination and promote good race relations between Africans and other communities.

Although based in Edinburgh, it covered Scotland. We even had our own office. It was quite small, but it was comfortable very central. Our work also involved promoting African cultures whenever we could.

We wanted people to know that we were there as active citizens and a force for good, ready to contribute into building a better place for all of us.

At the same time, I worked for the Edinburgh and Lothians Racial Equality Council. I worked with local councils, the police, communities, schools, colleges and the voluntary and community sector. I worked with people from the police.

A year later, I moved to another job in the Slough Race Equality Council, in the South East of England. It was a career progression.

I had more responsibilities than my previous job. I was the coordinator for a project of which objectives included providing assistance and advocacy to people who were victims of racial discrimination, cementing our position in influencing policy and policy making and development.

Three years later I moved to a more important role at Reading Council for Racial Equality as one of regional coordinator for a programme to work with black and minority ethnic organisations in the South East Region of England. It also involved supporting them to be more competitive and represent better the communities they serve. Most of my work at that time was more about policy than supporting individuals. I would help them apply for funding, maintain a strong policy position in their local areas.

I would also ensure that they were in positions that enabled them to scrutinise policies for the benefit of the communities they represented.

Part of my work also involved ensuring that black and minority ethnic communities were properly represented and were given a voice at the decision-making table.

I then move to work for BME Community Services in West Sussex, as Head of Policy and Programmes Development. A big chunk of my work involved policy work as well. But also making sure that we secure as much funding as possible to make sure that the organisation was able to meet its objectives.

During that time, I was also the executive editor for the "equality in action" magazine which obviously I researched and wrote articles, edited and publish them. I also manage some of projects and some of the people. I had big responsibilities in every aspect of the organisation.

I then got another job, as Prevent Training Engagement Officer, working for Crawley Borough Council, West Sussex County Council and Sussex Police.

Prevent was the UK Government's strategy to root out radicalisation and violent extremism. It was aimed at stopping people becoming terrorists or supporting terrorism. It had three objectives which included:

- challenging the ideology that supports terrorism and those who promote it,
- preventing people from being drawn into terrorism and ensuring that they are given appropriate advice and support; and
- work with sectors and institutions where there are risks of radicalisation that need to be addressed.

Part of my area of work was to deliver workshops to district to borough councils and county council, to the police, to communities, to housing organisations, voluntary and community sector organisation, NHS organisations and to schools.

It also involved raising awareness of the Prevent Strategy and worked with partners and communities to ensure that those who were susceptible to radicalisation and extremism were provided with the necessary support to get away from extremist ideologies.

Then I went back to university to do a master's degree in public health which is in some way an extension of all the kind of work I've done in the UK. It was a bit deeper than that. It involved health and well-being which obviously covered everything that I've done before. It's more about promoting good health physically and mentally.

At the same time, it's more all about promoting positive attitude and behaviour to health and wellbeing.

I finished, and I am now a public health community inclusion specialist and author. My passion for equality, diversity and inclusion continues. As a public health community inclusion specialist, some of my areas of interest include addressing health inequalities and promoting health inclusion.

In the process I wrote a book on prostate cancer for black men. The book addresses many issues including raising awareness of prostate cancer an issue that affect badly black men; encouraging black men to go and get screened as early as possible and suggesting an intervention and engagement model to challenge and change black men's attitude, assumptions and taboos towards prostate cancer and health and wellbeing in general.

One of my best experience of celebrating diversity happened when I worked for BME Community Services. We organised one of the best Black History Month events in the county that year. The event was well attended by a diversity of people that reflected the diverse communities of our local area.

We also invited a lot of professionals from different backgrounds. Our keynote speaker was a professor from Brighton University we also had representatives from the local councils, including the mayor and mayoress, colleges, the County Council Library. At the time we were running a project called out of Asia Project which was a project that talked about migration from the people from the Indian subcontinent. And that day was a very colourful day.

There were different types of food, music and people. The attendance was between 200 to 300 people in the club we hired for the event. It was such a happy event. People were happy and had real good fun.

Everybody was able to dance. Everybody was able to listen to their differing talks sound. I think it was one the greatest event I was involved in my professional career.

Such event really exemplifies what it means to celebrate diversity because in that room nobody was different from another person. Everybody was one and we were all working together, dance together, enjoy the event together.

Unfortunately, there are so many things that are happening around the world now that seems to raise suspicion and pointed fingers to the other. At times, the migrant is seen as the source of all problems in many countries, in Europe.

Another thing that has made situation difficult for migrants is the UK leaving the European Union. Since the referendum, racism has increased. Which is a worry. You can hear statements like, we want to take our country back; or we are swamped by many migrants.

Obviously, such discourse has not been very helpful for migrant communities. Statistics show that discrimination has increased, which increased worries. However, communities are confidents and resilient. They have matured enough to take part in the debate and repel any attitudes and behaviours likely to divide communities.

However, despite the current atmosphere, the UK is one of the best countries to live in for migrants. Fighting prejudice and celebrating Diversity will continue. There is a general understanding in the UK of the role diverse communities play and their contribution to building a UK that is prosperous and best for everyone who live here. you

THREE LESSONS ABOUT DIVERSITY
AND CELEBRATING DIVERSITY

*"We all tend to think diversity is a black
and white issue. It is not a black and white issue."*

Diversity is something that has been with us forever. In our families, we are not all the same. Nonetheless, we have grown to appreciate and respect our family members, although different from us. The same can be applied for our peers at work and at school.

Hating people because of their difference in characteristics we end up being the losers. Such attitude might lead us to miss out in our personal development, in the way we rise our children, in the way we want to achieve our goals in life.

You might also miss out in the way you interact with others. You might push away the person who might be able to help you progress in life because of the prejudice people carry with.

When we look around us, wherever at home or abroad, we will see that the world is heterogeneous and has always been. I think it time that people started to acknowledge that we are the human race. We come in different shapes and different colours. Nobody can ever change that.

Additionally, we celebrate diversity because of what it offers? Diversity brings harmony; diversity brings peace; diversity bring cohesion and inclusion and that's very important for the world.

The first step is to recognise that there are differences. The next stage is to try to understand how we make those differences work for all of us. for that to work, it is very important not to see those differences as a bad thing or something negative. It is not only a black and white or a man and a woman issue.

We all deserve our place in this world regardless of our characteristics. It is time we acknowledged that, for instance, in the workplace inclusive and diverse workforce works better. It is more creative innovative, and it benefits the organisation, therefore the society. If many organisations spend millions of pounds or dollars to implement a diversity and inclusive culture, it is because they know of the benefit it brings.

We live in a multicultural environment. It is a fact. So, it is very important for companies to make sure that they have a culture that is diverse and inclusive because an organisation can be diverse, but it doesn't necessarily mean it's inclusive.

It is important that organisations and leaders look at diversity in the workplace, and what they are doing to promote togetherness of the different types of people that they have in their organisation. And if that is not happening, they should ask themselves if they are making it a priority for them. Above all, diversity and inclusion in an organisation makes business sense.

For instance, in the city of Peterborough Council where we live their leadership forum has started looking at how they can be more inclusive and my partner has set up an awards appreciation system so that we can start appreciating those people that are celebrating diversity and inclusion.

Those people that are showing in their organisation in their day to day life that they are being inclusive. I am part and parcel of that award ceremony system.

We also ran three different courses together. One is "celebrating diversity and inclusion in the workplace". The other one is "cultural awareness and inclusiveness in society".

Obviously, it's not just about work; it's about the general society as well. If we want to live in harmony we need to be able to accept the diversity that is within our communities.

Thirdly, in my opinion, what stops people from being inclusive and celebrating diversity is hate crime. To address that, we are running a course that is entitled hate crime awareness and this course teaches people about how to identify and report hate crime; but also, how to help those people who experience any form of hate crime.

We are continuing to make sure that we challenge any issues that undermine efforts to promote diversity and inclusion in the community that we are living in.

I hope as you read this, you think about your own community and want to teach that you as an individual can contribute in a small or big part to your community and how you can continue to celebrate diversity.

Remember one thing. If you think you deserve to be treated with dignity and respect regardless of your characteristics, so does everybody else.

Angelinah Boniface

A mother, wife, daughter, sister, auntie and a friend. I consider myself a transformational leader, life coach and a trainer at heart. I am also a keen listener and learner.

My passion is to equip, guide, impart knowledge and skills to all those who are at crossroads in whatever part of their life journey, such that they can re-discover their passions and inner purpose. I believe that each one of us is here for a unique purpose. My journey is, therefore, to try to raise that deeper awakening within us, to align people with their life purpose and leave a fulfilling life, positively impacting communities. All this requires unique commitments from each one of us.

I cannot live another person's life, however, what is satisfying is seeing others go along their journeys with contentment and entertaining as big expectations as they deem possible.

Books and Publication include: (1) Co-Author of The Perfect Migrant (2) Contributor to Using Social Media in Libraries: Best Practices

Area of Expertise: Motivational Speaker, Human Rights Defender.

Speaking and Seminar Topics: Overcoming Your Shadow Vision.

Contact Details

Phone: +1 646 894 9964

Email: Angieakaboni1@gmail.com

Migration and Culture Preservation

By Angelinah Boniface

INTRODUCTION

"Migration is as natural as breathing, as eating, as sleeping. It is part of life, part of nature. So, we must find a way of establishing a proper kind of scenario for modern migration to exist. And when I say 'we,' I mean the world. We need to find ways of making that migration not forced."

-Gael Garcia Bernal

In less classical terms, migration is simply about the movement of people from one place to another in-country or across borders in search of economic opportunities or for any other reasons. When people move, more often than not they take with them their cultures. Thus the "baggage" of people on the move include; beliefs, language, food, customs, and social norms, amongst others. It is a way of life, a key distinguishing feature of groups of people, that's culture. I remember vividly when I went to Europe for the first time in 2007.

The excitement was exuberating, until I experienced this shock that almost shuttered my dreams. I was suffering from a self-diagnoses lack of exposure to the sun disease. The first few months were dark and heavy. Apart from my classmates and my roommate, I knew no one. I missed my life back home. I yearned for my mom's cooking, my weekends out in church with my friends and just laughing till my lungs complain in pain. I took with me my church regalia to the UK and some of the paraphernalia associated with a young lady in my culture. Though it took me some months to wear it in public what was important was that I had it with me. It is part of me. It is part of my culture. My culture is my identity.

Similarly, the Masai people of Kenya wear their cultural attire which distinguishes them from other tribes in Kenya and elsewhere. A Chinese in Beijing or elsewhere outside China would prefer to use chopsticks when eating let alone the preference of Chinese food. Americas at home as in America or away are fond of their fast food habits while the Italians and to some extent the Swiss would take time to sit, chat and drink their coffee or meals with no rush. Where I come from, eating out is luxury. I used to eat home-cooked dinner every night. I came to learn as an immigrant in Europe and the USA that, a home cooked meal is luxury.

As people migrate, cultures also migrate. Today, we talk of cultural diversity as different people co-exist in the global village. We also talk about cultural shock for those that are perplexed or those that cannot cope with other people's ways of living. We also talk of cultural tolerance when two or more cultures are juxtaposed, and the different people accommodate each other, and most important, live in harmony.

Apart from the above, there is talk of cultural integration and preservation. These two are closely linked to xenophobia and discrimination leading to two philosophical questions. Does cultural preservation by migrants lead to intolerance on the part of the host communities? Is integration the prescription against xenophobia and other anti-migrant tendencies displayed or likely to be exhibited host by people in their backyards? The proverb that: "when in Rome do as the Romans do" becomes relevant.

My story touches on a number of the elements flagged above that are within the migration-culture nexus. The story also includes dilemmas, uncertainties and identity crises associated with migration. I grew up within an environment that exhibited a combination of these variables as child of migrant parents in Moroka village in North East Botswana. I also have now experienced these issues as someone who is in the Diaspora as I interact with people of different nationalities and cultures. As a child born to migrants, I grew up under an identity crisis. Culture, so I believe, helped me in my later life to identify myself. When I was a young adult away from home, studying in the United Kingdom, I went through yet another struggle; that of preserving my culture against the temptation of abandoning it in a new environment.

EARLY LIFE: MY PEOPLE AND MY CULTURE

My parents met in Botswana after they had migrated from Zimbabwe. First to arrive in Botswana was my father, His Royal Highness Shadreck Mutero-Chandiwana in the early 1950s. My father was in his late twenties. His father, Gombwe Boniface Mutero-Chandiwana was a leader of a religious sect founded in eastern Zimbabwe, called the Gospel Church of Africa. It is locally known as Johane we Masowe. Before settling in Botswana, my grandfather together with his family and followers had been to Kenya, Zambia, South Africa and other parts of Southern Africa after leaving Zimbabwe in the 1940s. Theirs was a religious missionary voyage.

When my grandfather and his followers that included members of his extended family arrived in Moroka village in the early 50s, they were received with warm hands by the then chief of the village, Godfrey Moroka of Barolong. They were allocated land,

and they established a compound that still exists today in Moroka village. This is the place I call home. Most of my childhood was experienced in this Bazezuru compound until middle school. As migrants originating from present-day Zimbabwe, my people are referred to as BaZezuru by the locals. This emanates from their Shona language that has a very deep accent as compared to the locals. BaZezuru is not a tribe or a culture. It is a derogatory name given to these BaShona immigrants of Apostolic Religion from Zimbabwe. I will use BaZezuru here to refer to my people. As much as the BaZezuru name was derogatory, it didn't have much effect as compared to 'negro' for example.

The BaZezuru lived in a huge compound together and it is considered a holy compound. If you are not part of the church, you cannot stay in the compound. On Saturday, which is the designated Sabbath day, outsiders and non-followers of the sect are not allowed into the compound. In fact, the prohibition starts from 6 pm on Friday up to 6 pm on Saturday. The sect allows polygamy. My grandfather had four wives. Other men also have polygamous unions. I know of a distant uncle, a very close friend of mine, who has two wives. However, my father did not subscribe to polygamy hence he had my mother as the only partner in love, and he was very proud of himself for that. Polygamy was associated with wealth. The more the "wealth" you had, the more wives you would get.

The other practice in my sect was that sick congregants were not allowed to go to hospitals. These people were so religious that they believed only prayer can heal a person. True or not, it is neither here nor there. However, few people in the compound still subscribe to this belief. The majority are now sending sick people to hospital at the same time praying for them as they have embraced modernity.

Talking about hospitals, it was narrated to me that all of grandmother's seven children were born at home. I also witnessed mothers giving birth at home (in the compound) when I was a young girl in 1990s. As if that was not enough I also witnessed mothers hiding their new born babies whenever the health professionals were in the compound to administer vaccines to children.

The religious beliefs of the church also discouraged parents from sending their children to school. The fear was about perceived evil teachings from the school as the belief was we were the only holy a people. These are the people who were reading the bible. My question would have been, "where the bible came from?" Besides, bad omens were to come to the Bazezuru if their offspring were to be oriented in the other direction. I witnessed my cousins stay at home as I braced the winter going to school as a 1st grader. Thank, God my father disregarded the belief. He made sure that all his children went to school risking alienation from the Bazezuru community. Indeed, he was later on excommunicated.

In search of my identity

I was born in 1983 and brought up in an environment in which the Shona culture was followed away from Zimbabwe. This included peculiar religious practices that are still practised in Zimbabwe. As children, we played among ourselves in the compound with limited contacts with the outside world until I started going to school at the age of six. While at school, I began to formulate ideas in my "small brain". I became conscious that I and others from the compound were different from those who were coming from the rest of the village. Three elements preoccupied my mind.

First, we had our own language that was not spoken by the Tswanas. In the compound, we spoke mainly Shona. In fact, my grandfather only spoke Shona. He never bothered to learn Setswana. Shona is the main spoken by the majority of people in

Zimbabwe. To date, it is still widely spoken by the descendants of Bazezuru in Moroka though the young generation speaks Botswana local languages such Tswana, Kalanga and including Ndebele which is also spoken widely in Zimbabwe.

I speak fluent Shona (my mother tongue), Setswana, Sekalaka and Ndebele, the most spoken local languages. In the Bazezuru compound, it was about the Shona culture traditions and rituals when it comes to events such as marriage ceremonies weddings, funerals to mention a few. Most of these traditions are intertwined with religion.

Second, we had our own dress code. All Bazezuru especially girls, did not wear school uniforms. They wore religious attire which was predominantly white dresses and white head scarf. Remember, the regalia which were part of my baggage to Europe. It's a trade mark par excellence. Although bringing it to Europe had nothing to do with the religion of BaZezuru. As a young adult, I later got baptized in the Old Apostolic Church of Africa, which wears white on holy communion Sundays and other special occasions. This a story for another day.

The school principal and the teachers were not amused by the BaZezuru girls coming to school in religious regalia. It was always a war between the school and the church. At most, they would tolerate the white dress but not the headscarf. What girls would do is, wear the scarf from home and take it off in school. However, interestingly enough, I different from other girls from the compound. I had a school uniform. My father bought me a uniform. I did not have to wear the white dresses and the head gear since my father was long excommunicated from the church way before I started school.

My father used to say: *"my children, you should not be enslaved by religion. I want you to feel free. Religion shall not oppress you.*

Things are changing; we need to embrace change. Culture evolves and is dynamic". Of course, he said it in his vernacular language Shona. At that time in my child brain, I had no idea what he was talking about. Only thing I could see was someone trying to go against the norm. This probably gave me the strength I have today. I am my father's daughter.

Remember he was not a polygamist. He had embraced modernity by sending us to school and taking us to hospital whenever we fell sick. Rules should never be written on stone. People should never be put in a box.

Get rid of names and labels. Free their minds and them be. Too many rules when wrongly enforced enslave people. People need to be free, free from religion, intimidation or pressure. People need to be the best version of themselves without having to feel guilty or afraid of retaliation.

True to my father's sayings, he believed in an evolving human being. A culture that learns from its experiences. His vision was of a culture which adapts to the changing times and environment. However, he did not abandon his culture completely. Apart from telling us stories about where they came from occasionally, he would take us to our paternal and maternal relatives in Zimbabwe during school vacations. To this, I speak fluent Shona though I grew up in predominantly Tswana culture.

Thirdly, my last name. It was Shona. I later changed it to my grandfather's first name at seventh grade because it was "English" and easier to pronounce. My grandfather's other name was Hondzeri. This is the last name my sister and brother had used at primary school. I personally decided to use Boniface because of the poor pronunciation from the teachers and schoolmates. The fact that I was regarded as an alien gave me the strength at that early age to think seriously about my identity. Fast forward to today, if I knew what I know now, would I have changed it, probably, yes.

Growing up I was always curious about my identity. I wanted to find out whether I was Tswana or Zimbabwean. This was the foremost question among a number of questions that came into my mind while searching for my identity. The other questions were; does it matter to be an alien or a migrant? Is it a crime for my parents to be migrants? What distinguishes us from them?

It is the last question that led me to begin to interrogate our way of living in the compound versus their way of living outside the compound. The thinking processes took me to culture. Culture helped me to search for my identity and later to define myself let alone to preserve it after embracing it. Throughout my primary, secondary school education and higher education at University of Botswana, I was battling with the idea of discovering myself.

THE DIASPORA EXPOSURE: SMALL THINGS MATTER

I was an idealist when I moved to Sheffield the United Kingdom to pursue one-year postgraduate studies under the competitive Commonwealth Scholarship. I begin to see things different as travelled throughout Great Britain. First, it was the ever-green British countryside that was not only scenic but also breath-taking.

I used to read about things and places far away as a young girl. This time it was real. Sitting on the train from Sheffield to Luton, from Manchester to Cleethorpes, and one location place to another I always admired the countryside let alone the cities and towns in England. Apart from the adorable countryside, I turned the people and how they interact. I found them polite. I could hear them in trains, buses, restaurants, supermarkets and at the campus mentioning the words, "please, thank you and excuse me".

I came to know that the phrase: *"excuse me"* was, in fact, polite way of drawing someone's attention. Where I come from, *"excuse me"* is used when one is angry about someone. That's the way I understood it. Who knows, it could be a question of us back home having failed to grasp its proper meaning. Small things like this matter in new environment let alone when interfacing with a different culture.

The first time "excuse me" was used on me, was when I went grocery shopping for the first in the UK, at Tesco on Infirmary Road, Sheffield. As I went from isle to isle, every time someone went past me, there was "excuse me". My face would frown in shock. What did I do? It took only a few months until I joined in especially when on public transportation and restaurants.

I was amazed by the level cleanliness, order and the infrastructure in Britain, my first destination and experience in the diaspora as young adult who grew up 'encamped' in reference to the compound in Moroka village. I equate the compound to a refugee camp. That does not mean I had a bad childhood, or the camp was a bad place. In fact, I had the best experiences ever, growing up there. In Britain, there was no rubbish all over. People form queues in supermarkets, banks and bus stop, what I came to hear is referred to as the British Orderly. Everywhere, people were generally quiet and not screaming on top of voices. The music in all my places was played on low volume not playing too loud as what I was used to back home on weekends doing household chores. Of course, I missed that including the competition with neighbours of playing the best and too loud music on Saturday mornings. Not in Britain. I remember getting to school and experiencing the best-advanced infrastructure ever, from the InfoCommons to the Programming labs. Technology was moving in and it was coming fast. The internet worked faster and no scrambling for space.

I wished home was like this. I spent most of time in school and because everything worked so perfect, the InfoCommons so clean, I made it my second home.

I should not forget to share my first experiences with cold and harsh winters. The first winter was extremely terrible, but I survived. My bones quaked, my ears burned my hands numb. However, I made it. I did not mind the cold. It was the rain that kept me wondering; I did not understand why it rained all the time in Sheffield. In fact, I did not understand why we had like four seasons in a span of two hours.

One minute it was nice and sunny the next minute, it would be a combination of winds and rain. I had no idea what weather to dress for, winter, summer or rain if ever there is a season called rain. I understood why there was a warm clothes allowance with the scholarship. Instead of my buying enough warm clothes, I sent most of the money to my mother to care for my two children I had left with her.

The weather episode would not be complete without touching on footwear. Now I understand why the immigrants from Europe in my country loved to wear outdoor gear. To be honest, when it is winter, the most affected parts of body are the feet. I need to be putting on very warm shoes otherwise. It took me six years of living in the Diaspora to understand a good boot, like an Ugg. It has proved to be my salvation under the severe colds. It is very expensive though, but I have no choice if I am to survive in the winter especially in New York in the United States of America where I am based now. New York is colder than the UK.

Apart from the amazing and polite people, cleanliness, the 'British Orderly', the eye-catching infrastructure and the weather, there was the issue of food. To my utter surprise, I could not find my favourite foods. From one supermarket to another I hunted for the white maize meal that we used to cook thick paste-like mashed potatoes, and we call it palette in Setswana or sadza in Shona white maize meal porridge. This is my kind of food the tastic rice that I was used to back home. Never to be found. The beef was not tasty.

"The chicken was not like homegrown organic village chicken."

The chicken was even worse. It is not like the home (grown) raised chicken that is eaten in the village. The chickens roam over the yard. When you want to slaughter one you have to chase it all over the yard. For this reason, a chicken is called long-range or road runner. In Mozambique, they are known in Portuguese as "Galinha Murder Mutola" named after the female track runner and Olympic gold medallist Maria Matola. In Burkina Faso, the chicken in this category is called "bicycle chicken" or "poulet velo" in French. That was the chicken I was looking for. Now you understand my confusion at the supermarket when everyone seemed to be angry at me. I am angry because I cannot find my food.

Without the kind of food, I was used for everything was slowed down. Literally, even waking up was a problem my system could not be easily started I missed "sadza". I am not a rice person nor was a potato one. The UK food is flat and lacks flavour. I had to use a lot of spices and some flavours. However, as time went by I got used to some of the dishes. I remember, with my friend Thandy enjoying a bit of Yorkshire lunch comprised of roasted beef and potatoes with vegetables and gravy. Though to start, with gravy was difficult for me. I was delighted, later on, when I learned that there was a shop selling South African foods that is the same as what we eat back home. I would host parties with my friends from time to time at 123 Lichford Road where I stayed. African dishes were served and were popular with my friends some who are English.

CULTURE CONNECTION AND CO-EXISTENCE

My socio-cultural horizon began to expand when I joined my current employer the United Nations (UN) of which I have worked the past eight years in two duty stations. I have had the opportunity to live and work in New York, the United States and Geneva, Switzerland. The UN is an organization that embraces diversity and inclusion. I could not be more grateful to work in an environment where all people from all corners of the world are in the corridors and all working for a great course. I thought I had an accent when I was in Sheffield, that all ended when I came to the UN headquarters in 2010. All accents are welcome here. You even hardly notice the differences in us. We celebrate diversity and embrace all cultures. The Africa week is one of those events that speak to diversity in the UN. We share food and culture during the commemorations. I have come to realize that the majority people in the Diaspora have not abandoned their cultures. Indeed, they preserve it.

This, however, does not mean that they are not integrated in their respective communities. Some are solidly integrated. Integration does not entail or lead to culture abandonment. Integration speaks to culture co-existence, it speaks to the respect of other people's way of living. There is nothing that brings happens in my heart than knowing that what I do here, no matter how little, it will benefit a person in need and make a difference in their life. My concentration is not only in Africa, but my impact is also where I am right now. Impacting the community starts with where I live and where I am raising my children whether in Sheffield, the New York, Geneva or Gaborone. Integration is possible and should be embraced. Diversity is beautiful and should be embraced. This is how my children now are fluent in both English and French. My daughter struggles with Shona, but she understands it when

I speak to her slowly. My wish would have been for her to know Shona as well. However, since I am the only one who speaks with them, they don't hear it anywhere else around them unless in Botswana, my daughter found it weird even to learn it.

Having lived and worked in three different continents, I can strongly say, diversity is the best tool we have at our disposal. From food, music, dress to weather, we all have different ways of experiencing life, and sharing that the joy is the best thing ever. With all the negative dogma on migration, we all need to get to the centre of our being and realize that sharing joy is all we have to attain the best versions of ourselves. There is joy in sharing cultures. Choose Joy, Choose kindness. Build a bigger table instead of building walls. Life will meet you where you are. Take the chance, embrace and trust the process, travel the world and spread kindness

THE AMAZING LANGUAGE AND NORMS

Before concluding my story and sharing where I stand now, I need to share some experiences and moments that are not far away from what I have shared so far about myself within the purview of migration-culture nexus. When I moved to Geneva from New York, the initial months were a nightmare simply because of the language. My kids and I knew no French, German or Italian the languages spoken in Switzerland.

In the UK and New York, the language is English, and its one of my languages as Botswana was under the British during the colonial era. I remember shortly after arriving in Geneva going to enrol my daughter at school. None of the administrators spoke English except the Principal who could pick here and there some English words. A process of registration that ordinarily takes a few hours took close to half a day. We simply could not understand each other most of the times.

The Suise are very particular about who they bring into their inner spheres. You are either Suise, or you are not. Driving around in the beautiful Suise villages, I could feel a sense of emptiness. No one looks like me here, no one understands me here, how I will survive. Even lost, I was afraid to ask for directions. One day my phone dies before I got to my destination that meant I had no GPS. I drove for almost half an hour looking for a place that was only four minutes away from the place my GPS died. I was scared to ask for directions. I didn't know German let alone Suisse German.

The experience motivated me to keep my daughter in Swiss public schools throughout my stay in Geneva. By the time we left Geneva after three and half years my daughter was fluent in French. I also went for French lessons for it was important to communicate in the local language in shops and in most of the public places. My daughter still takes French lessons in New York. When we left Geneva, coming back to New York, my daughter had started German lessons.

At a session with my Physical Therapist (**PT**), **I had an encounter that resonates with the issues forming part of this conversation and** worthy sharing. It is about my accent. Not until this encounter I never knew that my accent could be an issue of note to anyone.

The conversation went as follows;

PT: You have a cool accent, where are you from?

Me: Moroka Village

PT: Which State is that? Is it in Colorado...

Me: No, it's in Botswana, Southern Africa.

PT: oooh, South Africa... I hear Oprah is from there; she built a school there right.

Me: No. Botswana is a country. And my accent is from Rockville aka Moroka Village.

PT: It's cool. I like it. You have been here that long, and you haven't lost your accent? It sounds British. I thought you are British.

Me: No ma'am, I am a Zezuru... 😂😂😂😂

PT: Oooh nice.... (You should have seen her face).

I expected her to ask me more questions, but she didn't. I think she was more confused more than anything. Unfortunately for me as well, I wasn't sure if I had to volunteer explaining what I meant by a Zezuru. I am sure my next session will be very interesting with her. I love my Americans. Certainly, people's accents are matters associated with migration and diaspora conversations. One's identity is not necessarily dependent on the accent. I concluded after the encounter with the therapist. 😂😂😂😂

Interestingly, my former hosts, the Suisse are fond of following the rules by the book and are very much regulated society. No noise from 10 pm to 7 am. Notices to this effect are everywhere in the apartments. I think the next thing to be regulated will be showering and flushing of toilets. I can imagine notices to the effect that no opening of the shower taps or flushing of toilets between 10 pm and 7 am.

The Suisse are particular and want to follow the regulations to the letter without exceptions or shortcuts. No noise and no parking in wrong spots or the police will show up at your house. One evening I forgot to park my car in the designated bay in the basement of my apartment building. In fact, I had parked my car outside apparently on another tenant's parking bay, rushing to my apartment hoping to return in minutes as I had to drive out take a friend for an outing. While I was in my apartment, the friend called to cancel our appointment. Without thinking about the car, I decided to relax in the couch. I then slept, and when I woke up after a two-hour nap on the couch, I dragged my tired body to the bedroom and slept.

At 2:26 am I woke up to a terrifying knock on my door. It was so, so, loud that I thought we were under attack or there was fire outbreak. I listened and heard..."police". I rushed to the door with my heart beating very fast and sweating, I almost collapsed. I my dizzy state, first I checked my children's rooms, everyone was fast asleep. I wondered what it was. After checking if it was "real police" at the door, indeed it was, I opened the door.

Police: Ms Boniface

Me: oui (yes) in my little just acquired French.

Police:..... voiture?(meaning car) The policeman said a few more lines before the voiture, I just didn't hear, either his French was too deep or was still in a sleepy mode.

I just heard...."voiture" meaning car.

Me: basement

Police: (in French accent) you parked in someone's parking space. Remove your car.

Me: no (I could not remember)

Police: oui

You should have seen me rushing to go pick up my keys and racing downstairs to remove my car. As I got down, not only where there my neighbours' car, but two police cars. People in Switzerland call police if you park in someone else's bay. Whereas in Africa, if yours is occupied you find an alternative bay or space elsewhere to park your car.

The Police can't be bothered about parking bays. So the Swiss Police after receiving the complaint had to contact the Vehicle Registration department to get my details including the apartment number. After my neighbours arrived from their outing, they could not risk parking their car anywhere. While they were still figuring out what to do, apparently another neighbour called the police to report people idling in the parking lot. Hence two police reported to the scene. The ones who reported me for parking in their bay, and the ones who reported them for idling at 2 am in the building parking lot. The Swiss are amazing.

Where do I stand now as I conclude?

Earlier in the chapter, I alluded to the fact that culture helped me to discover myself. Indeed, it helped but in combination with the Diaspora exposure. Away from home, I have never abandoned the way things are done by my people back in the village. My appetite for African food is still there. My love for African fashion is growing. I feel myself when donned in African attire. I have a colleague who calls me, Ms Africa. I believe this is because of the African attires I wear at the office.

I am still religious just like I was growing up in the compound. I still respect the African traditions, and I am even introducing my two children to the African norms and customs though they have grown up away from home. While they speak English and French, I encourage them to learn our local language Tswana. They even appreciate part of the Shona language that is my mother tongue.

I have managed to discover myself. The identity crisis is over. I now know who I am. I now know where I stand and how I relate to the people in Moroka village which is my home. However, it took for me to be away from home to be able to provide answers to the questions that were a concern to me while growing up, being labelled an alien when in fact I was born and bred in Moroka village.

More importantly, I discovered that culture is about identity, it defines a person, a people and community and that cultural diversity is a key pillar of the global village that we live in today. At the same time, there is a new wave of culture we all need to embrace; we are all human before anything else. We feel the same way, we love the same way, and we are one. We all have the same need, to be the best version of our self and to be heard. Boundaries and silos or cultures may set us apart but we all interconnected. The connection that transcends colour, race, religion or region.

Savithri Jayaweera

I am an Integrative Psychotherapist. I work from the premise that we all carry the wisdom within us to know what is best for our progress and development. I am a qualified Clinician & I have completed Postgraduate studies in clinical psychology/Integrative Counselling/Psychotherapy with clinical experience. I have completed my DiPhil (Phd) research & my area of work is Domestic Violence, Sexual abuse, HIV/AIDS, BME Communities, Children, Young people & Families.

To complement my practice I have trained in an Integrative model, which is Psychodynamic, Person centred, Gestalt, TA & Cognitive Behavioural Therapy (I mainly practice MCBT techniques which identify and target destructive thought patterns which have a negative impact on our emotions & behaviour and Transpersonal Therapy skills, which place our spirituality and soul as central to our experience). I am also trained in EMDR.

I am a practitioner for Youth service, YMCA(Specialized in Children, Young People & Families). I have long term experience working at Black, Minority Ethnic Community Services as a BME practitioner & a Project Co-coordinator.

I also work with other referral agencies such as NHS, Addactions & The Women's Hub.

Books Inclulde: Celebrating Diversity

Area of Expertise include: Culturally sensitive Psychological assessments/ Counselling/Consultation service tailored to all ages, BME communities, Children, Young people & Families.

Contact Details:

Facebook: WAMEE: https://www.facebook.com/waminorityethnic/

Diversity and Cast Systems

By Savithri Jayaweera

INTRODUCTION: MY HISTORY.

I was born and brought up in Colombo in Sri Lanka. I had a relatively good childhood. I had a good education and family that look you know supported me and came from a family of professionals. My parents did get divorced when I was about 11. However it didn't affect me as much as you know to a level that my whole life fell apart and it was always understood that I would finish my A-levels and I'll come to the UK to join my mum.

Because around the early 90's, my mother moved to the UK, and she trained as a nurse. So, I think early 2000's, about 2000 and 2001, I moved to the UK to pursue my higher education and obviously join my mom. So that was always something that I knew I was going to do. I grew up in the city.

Colombo is the capital of Sri Lanka. It's immensely diverse. My neighbours, I had Sri Lankan Malays, Tamils, all sorts of people who were our neighbours, our family friends. Because my family members came from different walks of life in terms of their professional backgrounds. We had lots of family friends, and an Asian cultures are often quite extended. So we have lots of dinners, lunches.

We've celebrated everything under the Sun. There's lots of festivals. So there was, I think Sri Lanka at the time had a little bit of tension in terms of the ethnic conflict between the Sinhalese and the Tamils. But it was more of a political conflict. We celebrated our festivals together with everyone else. We loved our cricket. So that was something, everyone, regardless of the ethnicity or the cultural background that they came from. We all get together to celebrate a good game of cricket.

MY ARRIVAL IN THE UK

Arrived when I was about 19 years old in 2001.

I have been to the UK prior to coming here to settle down. Because my mother, she's been here since 1993 I think. So, I've been here for holidays. I was aware of West Sussex. I think West Sussex wasn't as diverse. It wasn't as diverse as it is now. But I was pleasantly shocked. London and areas around London they are quite diverse. You will see lots of different ethnicities. But West Sussex in particular wasn't that diverse at the time. So coming from a city Colombo buzzing, it felt as if I was coming to the god's waiting room.

Lot of old people. It was beautiful. It was very green. It was a lovely County in terms of the beauty and definitely one of the English Rivera's or whatever they call it. But I think for young people, being a young person at the time I was so glad to see a coloured face. It was like, wow I'm seeing a coloured face. They are more diverse now. 18 years, 19 years. But you know back then it was difficult. If you want to see quite a lot of diversity, the best place to go was the learning hospital. Because all the doctors and nurses were quite foreign or the corner shop, the curry shop or the corner shop or the Indian restaurants. Indian restaurants, but all of them were Bangladeshi restaurants.

CELEBRATING DIVERSITY IN PROFESSIONAL LIFE

In my professional life. I think that's where I was far more celebrating diversity. Because a lot of people within the NHA or the charity sector, I think I met you early, at the early stages of my internship. Black and Minority Ethnic Community Services (BMECS) in 2008. When I was doing my internship. So I think my journey obviously started off from there and we did quite a lot of you know the women's group and other activities.

So, we tried to bring people together and promote diversity. Within the profession I think I could see more diversity because of the professionals who were in the NHS or the community sector. They wanted that. I suppose there have been quite a number of events and you know functions that we have organized when the BMECS was around and also other community groups as well probably. Yes I suppose it's still a long way to go though.

BMECS was the only charity at the time came that was promoting support for black minority ethnic communities and the only one in the west Sussex and the So that was quite a lot of responsibilities and you know taking that message out into the community. The project out of Asia, the Black History Months, the events and I think BBC children in need, what else we did? The women's group that we used to have every two weeks or once a week. So out of Asia was one of the biggest projects I remember I was involved in. because it was the Chester University, the County Council and the Black and Minority Ethnic Community Services (BMECS). So, it was a human story of migration to the West Sussex. Which was quite a poignant moment as well. Because I did some of most of the interviews and was part of the whole process. So that was a very interesting experience.

WHY DIVERSITY IS SO IMPORTANT TO ME

Why do I get involved in organizations that promote Diversity?

I suppose I think I did pick up a gap. Because West Sussex wasn't as diverse as the other areas of like London or Crawley could be. So, I noticed there was a gap and there was a cultural imbalance and the people can very easily be isolated. Migrants could be very easily isolated. I picked up on it and I realized being a migrant myself and coming from a very vibrant community.

I missed that part in my life and I want to be a part of it and promote it. Particularly around mental health as well. Because these things can have a major impact on a person's, you know identity, mental health side of things. When you're not connected with your own community and those are things that give us a little bit of nourishment and belonging of culture. So I picked up on it and I wanted to do something about it, and it gave me my own spiritual and cultural nourishment as well.

Why is it that important to you having that nourishment and having that you know like relating?

You are in a different country, from your country of birth.

THE IMPORTANCE OF ACKNOWLEDGING
AND CELEBRATING DIVERSITY

It is a very important part of human life. Your identity is formed by the culture and the communities that you belong to. It is important, and regardless I suppose in the UK, Sri Lanka was a British colony. Sri Lanka was is actually a Portuguese, Dutch and a British colony. For 500 years, I think British rule about 300 years. We are somewhat familiar with the British Way of life, and we've got lots of souvenirs and monuments all around Sri Lanka, you know the poignancy of the being a Commonwealth country as well.

I wasn't as if I dismissed the whole English culture. I was aware, and I was far happier to embrace all of that. But I was also quite mindful of my own upbringing, my own set of values and morals and my culture. Because that is an important part of my life and it gives you that confidence. When you are confident in your own shoes, you are confident as a person so. I always say I've been here 18 years now.

I always say Sri Lanka gave me my identity, who I am, and England gave me my existence. Because when I came from Sri Lanka to the UK, I was in my late teens, 19 years old and then I moved on to college and university in the UK.

I completed my primary and secondary school in Sri Lanka and the University and higher education over here. So my existence and my character came out through those professional developments, and so you know both countries have made me who I am today, and you know I'm eternally grateful for that, and it is important to acknowledge that. It's not one or the other. But it is about celebrating the best of both worlds.

CELEBRATING THE BEST OF BOTH WORLDS.

My opinion is that at the moment, there many issues around negativity which undermine celebrating diversity. Especially, with all the issues in relation to migration, it seems to centre a lot on where people come from and less on what contribution they are making to the country they are living in.

There is also the divisive issue of Brexit. You know when people are seeking asylum and immigration is not seen in a very good way and much as diversity shouldn't really be linked to immigration, it is in a way. Because when you talk to people about diversity, what you hear most is more the migration-related diversity.

What is the biggest problem in the world today around people accepting diversity?

I suppose it comes with understanding and there's an element of ignorance as well. When there are these conflicts around Brexit or religious issues or cultural issues. It often stems from something to do with ignorance and lack of understanding. Because if we respect each other's believes and if we are happy to find a middle ground, there's no place by ignorant. But it's because either one party feels that they haven't been acknowledged while the other, that's where the tension comes in and that happens quite a lot in the community and a lot of the times not many people, there are certain people who are very well-travelled and they see other cultures, and they are able to embrace; the links and the differences. But many people aren't.

Because I suppose then certain crowd in the UK would see immigrants coming into the UK is a burden on the United Kingdom. Because of benefits and those things and they might not be contributing towards that there. But actually that's not the case. There's a lot of immigrants who are contributing to the economy of the country. The NHS is a very good example. Other private sectors or government sectors.

It's a lack of knowledge and ignorance that creates this tension. I suppose as immigrants when you're coming into another country, as the old saying goes when you are in Rome do as the Romans say or do as the Romans do. It is important to ponder on that. You don't have to do a makeover of your own identity completely. It is crucial to try join in and understand the other culture as well.

We live in the UK, this is the Western culture. Our culture is the culture is good as well, and this is the way that we think, and this is how I think it should work, if we are to live in harmony with other people. You need to find the best of both worlds and there's always good and bad in both sides and but for me personally, I've got a son now, who's born and brought up here.

He has Asian roots. He is from a mixed-race marriage. But he is obviously you know he's got Asian roots. But he's born and brought up here and if you ask him to do you feel Sri Lankan or do you feel your father's you know culture. He would say I am British, I was born here. So, but at home we would try to make him aware of the culture and the background that he comes from. But for him, it's what he, it's comfortable for him. So, to him. He would say well this is the culture that I know. I don't think there's anything wrong with it.

HAVING A MIXED-RACE SON

How that's read in my community?

My son is of mixed heritage; he's super confident in his identity. He's Asian mixed race. His father is Pakistani, and I am Sri Lankan. That brings its own challenges with the two strong cultural backgrounds. I think one of the challenges I have faced is not actually within my community, but across the two. People would say things like; *"so do you speak both languages. Do you speak Sinhalese and do you speak Urdu."* It is funny when Sayyam turns, and he says I speak neither, I can speak in English, French and Spanish.

They look at me almost like with disapproval or a level of disgust at the shame I must be bringing to them. And then they ask me questions like… *"why have you not taught your mother language or why have you not taught him his father's language?"*

This is interesting to me because I've always said we speak in English at home, even when I was in Sri Lanka, my family dis speak English as well as our own language. I have often spoken to him in English; Not that I have to qualify why their views don't matter but for the sake of explaining the barriers we sometimes put on ourselves. These are some of my reasons. It's good for children to learn various a variety of languages and he's a very quick learner so why not I ask.

Some people, especially the men are very quick to ask; *"So, when you go to Sri Lanka, how do you speak to the people there? How do you communicate with the family?* Sayyam looks at them and says, *"they all speak English. So, they speak to me in English."*

It hasn't really been a problem for us in terms of you don't. Because just because a person speaks some mother tongue, doesn't necessarily make you a better culturally influenced person. I don't believe that personally. A languages is a good language. I speak several other languages other than Sinhalese. Several other Asian languages. But that's because I was interested in it. It doesn't make me a lesser Sri Lankan or a Sinhalese.

I say I didn't really bother about getting him to learn about Urdu or Sinhalese. I was moving in terms of morals and values and being you know being a better human being. It can be challenging. You are sometimes put on the spot, oh you're useless. You don't speak either of the languages of your parents and he is quite resilient to bounce back instead of thinking, oh that's a negative comment towards me. He would laugh, and he said well I speak English. You understand what I'm talking to you.

We fail to celebrate and appreciate other cultures if we are so set in our own ways. People have lived in the UK over 40 years and yet they do not speak English. Isn't it the reason why there is so much forcing of integration. If we made efforts on our own to speak the language that is the country where we live now. We would be more likely to see the beauty of being part of the wider community.

I know some people with think this is controversial, but it is a fact.

He hasn't necessary experienced bad cases of racism because he has a great network of friends who stand up for him. I don't think there has been elements of racism as such in school or in terms of him not having opportunities. The moment, he hasn't had that so far. However, I remember one incident and when he was in primary school, he wasn't only in year one or so he was a little five-year-old or a six-year-old and they were playing in the school ground.

So, this is a good example of diversity actually even among children and how innocent kids can be. He was playing with his best friend Riley and another boy, I think Fred. Fred and Riley in the playground and a boy from year three kept following Sayyam and started calling him chocolate sundae and Sayyam actually didn't understand what chocolate sundae means.

He just thought this boy is just being annoying. So, he just literally kept following Sayyam. It was the first school, primary school around the playground and the two friends who are white British; they got annoyed for Siam, and they started pushing this boy away and said go away, go away. You know don't trouble my friend. So that's diversity.

That is standing up for your friend. They didn't know what chocolate sundae means. They didn't know there was a racial connotation to it. They just protected their friends. I think the teachers then picked up on it and they were very ashamed of it and they called us, and they said, we're really sorry something like this has happened. We've spoken to the boy and his parents, and he's got a couple of detentions at the moment and you know we then had to have a conversation with Sayyam about what this means and I think that was a very important conversation, which gave him the stepping stone of understanding his own identity and to be comfortable in that and with regards to the other boy, I have a lot of empathy towards the young child.

Because it's not something that he's aware of. It's something he's picking up from his family or from the community that he belongs to and he thinks it's all right to have somebody or bully somebody by saying that. He got a note after that from the boy apologizing. So, I suppose it starts from home and the diversity often starts from home and the lack of resilience to experience other people's cultures and you know embrace that is what creates this lot of these frictions among people in terms of fear and not knowing the unknown. Do not want to come out of the little box that they're in and see the world outside. I mean I'm somebody who loves to go to church. I'm not even a Christian. I like to go to the mosque during the Ramadan time. Because it's very spiritual. I've got other friends like the Baha'is, and I love you know mingling around these communities and friends, and I love the food and the company.

I like singing in a choir. Because I like singing. I don't have to be a Christian to sing in a choir necessarily. I just like gospel singing. It's about learning. I think embracing cultures and different things stems from my childhood in Sri Lanka. We were quite diverse as a family. We would celebrate each other's festivals like my grandmother. She studied in a convent, in a Methodist convent.

She would always singing at home, and although we never converted, I think every two weeks we would go to the Saint Anthony's Church and light a candle. We are not Christians. However, it's good practice, and it is an unbiased a way of being you know. It is embracing something nice. When Ramadan comes along we celebrate some days with the friends. We also have lots of Sri Lankan and Malay family and friends who observe different religions. We get to enjoy lovely food when they would invite us to their events. I loved it. I love celebrating Diversity that way.

I think I carried some of those traits to West Sussex with me. Though I must say it was a was culture shock when I arrived in Worthing and to find it is more God's waiting, not that it's a bad thing have its own way of life, such as shops closing early and not having much of a night scene despite the fact that it is a seaside resort.

Lessons to Share

What lessons can I share with somebody who feels quite negative about going across their own culture?

It doesn't make me a lesser Buddhist just because I go to the St. Anthony Church and light a candle. It's just a form of respect and embracing what's good in the other religion or the other culture. If you're afraid of know about other people, if you're afraid of even learning about other religions or cultures, that is an internal barrier you are putting on yourself and you are missing out on a lot.

However, I appreciate that it is a process that each person has to go through. My advice is that you need to push those boundaries a little bit. It doesn't mean, it's not a sin, nor anything to go and be a part of another festival or a cultural or you know say a prayer.

There's nothing wrong in that. But it doesn't make you a lesser person. I think it's a person's internal process and a lot of people who are actually very spiritual and who are very religious, they wouldn't be fearful of doing those things. Because they know it doesn't make them a lesser person.

It is the ones who are less informed and who aren't very comfortable in terms of their own identity who are worried about learning you know about the other religions or cultures. To criticize another person's belief system, you first need to learn about it. Without learning about it, you can't criticize and the more you learn you realize you're actually not criticizing, you're actually having a constructive conversation or sharing constructive feedback.

There's a big difference between sharing constructive feedback and criticizing somebody's belief system. I think we should all be encouraged to have open and honest conversations without the political correctness.

CHALLENGING NORMS AND NOTIONS IN SOCIETY

"Peer pressure and social norms are powerful
influences on behaviour, and they are classic excuses."
- Andrew Lansley

Norms and social influences are very powerful indeed. I suppose you need follow some of them in order to be 'accepted'. However, it is no surprise that when a very small pretenders who associate themselves to a certain culture do wrong, you all get coloured with the same paint brush. You know one of the most important 'elephant in the room' situations that are going on in this society at the moment is Islamophobia.

A few people have made some of society's ignorant people think the whole of the Muslim community are bad. Now, I am not Muslim, but I know a lot for people from the Muslim community and I feel Before you blatantly criticize Islam, you just have to learn about it first.

There's so many sects and so many cultures and so many different ways people practice it. So, it's about you need just need to be more mindful and learn about these things than you know labeling somebody with a certain tag, and also that's one thing that because of this Islamophobia. But then the recent events in Burma as well which took place, their human rights were involved.

You just need to learn about what's actually, it's not Buddhists are killing the others. It's a political issue. So you need to know what is actually going on in the country and before telling let's strip somebody's Nobel Prize, I don't know it just sounds very controversial. However, it's about learning what the issue is before you actually go and criticize somebody else or someone else's belief system.

AVOID FOLLOWING BLINDLY

"Rather than following blindly, gaining an understanding and education before you make your decision will help you appreciate people who are different from you."
- Amina Chitembo

There are certain situations where people just don't want to celebrate diversity that's surround, and they'll keep fighting it for the rest of their lives. If they learn about it, if they learn about whatever it is that they against and they still feel they would rather not change their way of thinking, that's okay.

At least they are making an informed decision. Where rather than just following blindly. Because my ancestors were this race and I can't talk to those people or because I was born in this sector this culture, then I can't talk to people like that.

Because there's no one pure race. We are all in terms of DNA we are all mixed. So, it's just how people sometimes want to identify. That's what own ego. That's to satisfy their own ego that they want to say. I mean I would say yes, I'm Sri Lankan origin. But it is not something I can deny. I am Sri Lankan origin and I'm proud about that.

However, that doesn't mean I would go and criticize someone else's cultural you know believes. I would love to learn more, and the education is very important. Because when there's education or you know developing your knowledge, there's less room for ignorant. Because a lot of these conflicts come through ignorance and lack of understanding. So that is quite important.

WHAT I DO FOR WORK

I'm a clinical psychotherapist. I practice as a psychotherapist. I started off being an intern and with the BMECS. I specialised in working with people from ethnic minority communities and then

I moved on to work with children and young people with Sussex central YMCA as a psychotherapist and I am now working for the early intervention and prevention team within the West Sussex County Council with young people. Supporting them with their needs and youth emotional support assessments and sessions.

A family work working with the whole families. It's a very; it can get very stressful. But it is also a very rewarding profession. Because you learn quite a lot. The complexities of life, the complexities of relationships and how human mind works, how human beings operated within relationships and so it's tremendously enriching field of work. However, due to the nature of work, listening to other people's issues, it can get stressful as well.

Outside of that work, you know because I always love my community work I always want to work with the minorities. That's where my heart is as much as you know doing the general psychotherapy work. I think once I left BMECS. I always wanted to do something in the same line from there onwards. BMECE which was founded by Amina Chitembo was an organisation within West Sussex coastal strip. Later I reached out to my dear friend and my colleague Amina who was the CEO for BMECS. I asked her to help me set up a similar organisation.

The need is there in the community, but charity sector is very complicated, very difficult. So, I wasn't talking about doing a charity. I wanted to do some work around community work with my experience. So, I've got a lot of support from her and you know other people who are involved with the work. And I just started off a little Community Interest Company. I don't know whether that's what it's called, or community group called Worthing and Adur Minority Ethnic Empowerment. It's mostly to do with mental health side of work. So general mental health well-being, psychological assessments workshops for Black and Minority Ethnic

(BME) communities and you know influencing the professionals who work with the BME communities.

That's my main aim. There's a lot of professionals. They are working with the BME people. But they don't actually know the psyche of how to work with them. so it's about you know giving them that training in terms of these are some of the challenges you would come across and how you can work with them cohesively. So, we started it in 2015. It was a bit quiet at the early stages until we get got a little bit of funding. Luckily, we got some funding and we started the work now and we have so far done three workshops. Which is the BME mental health workshop for professionals. The Female Genital Mutilation workshop and safeguarding and the International Women's Day and in between there have been psychological assessments and counselling sessions for BME people.

WHY I HELP PEOPLE FROM ETHNIC MINORITY COMMUNITIES WITH MENTAL HEALTH ISSUES.

"The equal right of all citizens to health, education, work, food, security, culture, science, and wellbeing, the same rights we proclaimed when we began our struggle, in addition to those which emerge from our dreams of justice and equality for all inhabitants of our world - is what I wish for all."
- Fidel Castro.

Because I see a lot of gaps within the West Sussex. I've seen our communities, like BME communities falling through the nets. They are not picked up by the NHS or the Primary Care Trust or the mental health teams. They seem to fall through the nets because professionals do not know how to address these issues and also the BME communities would take a step back. Because they think that the professionals don't understand. there is a real gap in service provision. There's a huge gap. Even through my work with young people, I see it all the time.

I see far less BME young people coming as referrals and even if they are being referred to camps or self-referral to us, they don't often engage because of the stigma attached. There is a lack of education on the types of services available. There is also a perceived reluctance to access services that are linked to mental health.

The other communities, like the wider communities they don't access the services because there's a language barrier. There's a cultural barrier. So, they struggle. They struggle a lot and I remember when I was working with domestic women who were involved with domestic violence, they did not know where I come from or anything.

All they recognised me was a time brown skin and that was more than enough for them to start off that conversation. Unfortunately, I spoke a common language that was understandable to them. So that reduced the gap. That reduced the tension between us. Because language is very important. So I think for them it was the familiarity of realizing okay this person, although I did not understand what the issue was. But that initial that was quite helpful.

THE LINK BETWEEN ETHNIC MINORITY PEOPLE NOT ACCESSING SERVICES AND THEM CELEBRATING DIVERSITY

There is a difference between celebrating diversity and clinical work. When I think diversity is a community gathering. So, they would love to participate in community events celebrating their culture or their festivals. Because there's no stigma attached in it. When it comes to clinical diagnosis and clinical work, domestic violence or therapy; there are lots of barriers there. The cultural understanding, the language, the stigma; all of that. So diversity is more of a gentle factor in that sense. Because they are coming to celebrate in their own culture. But when it comes to clinical settings, it's a different uniform all together.

For people to celebrate that the fact that we live in a diverse world, they have to feel included.

THE INCLUSION ASPECT OF DIVERSITY

Diversity requires commitment. Achieving the superior
performance diversity can produce needs further action - most
notably, a commitment to develop a culture of inclusion.
People do not just need to be different; they need to be
fully involved and feel their voices are heard.
- Alain Dehaze.

The way diversity could help inclusion is that when people are included in these cultural activities, community events, and in the clinical settings. People seeing that you are brown skin and a mental health professional can help, it can make it easier for them to come and talk to you.

What if you were not brown skin and you are a psychotherapist that's running that organization, how would that affect?

I hope is that the first impression is; we are similar so you to going to understand issues better and because you get my culture. People always want to be understood. Understand where I'm coming from, and for someone who comes from an Asian background, they think that you have a knowledge about how that culture functions or what these issues. So for me getting the specialisation was important because it helps me to navigate some of the issues that my clients come with.

I must say that most of the psychotherapists, they do not unless you specialize in that area of work, most of the clinicians or the psychotherapists do not have training around cultural diversity. So, it's a difficult side for them as well. Because they are getting to know someone else's issues through a different perspective and when the transference comes into it, their perspectives and the client's perspectives can clash at times. If you have the cultural awareness, it makes it easier for that transference to be strong.

"We all choose what career path we take, right?"

You chose to be a psychotherapist. Other people chose to be doctors and within your career, there are people from ethnic minority background. But there are people from Native communities as well. In this case they're British people. But at the end of the day when you are employed to your work, you are not employed based on your cultural background. So, taking that back to our communities as to ethnic minority communities, what lessons would you give to the communities. Because it feels to me a bit like we would suffer because we do not trust the profession who is not the same colour as us.

That is why it is very important for the professionals to have that training around diversity. Because a lot of the professionals don't. The ones who do have the training around diversity or cultural awareness, they wouldn't have a problem of connecting with your patient or with your clients.

Professional Judgement and Our Communities

Is the problem with the professional or is it that we are judging them? As minority communities we may be judging the profession before we even go and access the service.

That barrier is also there. That is true. That barrier is actually is there. If you meet the professional, let's say you push the barrier a little bit and you're going for your first consultation meeting, and if the professional as well have that cultural awareness and the training around diversity, they know which step to start with. When you don't have that awareness, it's very difficult it's about coming down to their level.

Sometimes I do have a different way of speaking with my clients, if I know I'm talking to a person from the ethnic minority backgrounds and they have a difficulty of language or you know expressing themselves. There are different ways that I could use my skills to stick down to that person's needs and that comes through that awareness and training as well. I suppose there's bit of both sides.

It's our community sometimes having preconceived thoughts and negative emotions towards the system and whether they are going to understand this or not and also the professionals as well, who are coming from that background. If they don't have that awareness that can really clash quite a lot and you wouldn't get appropriate support.

With the professionals first. Let's start with the professionals. What three things would you advise a professional who is helping an ethnic minority person, for them, it will help them to feel comfortable. What are the three things that you think are important that are must for the professionals.

> *"It is the empathy, the congruence and that positive regard that make the work worth it in any profession."*

Because especially in a setting like the General Practitioners (GP). Where lots of ethnic minorities are bound to go to see their GP's. It's about even if you don't have the cultural awareness, it is having those non-judgmental views and perspectives and if you feel that this needs to be assessed a bit further, then refer them to a person who can do that means assessment and take it from there.

We have to show non-judgmental views empathy towards the person. If the person has got language barriers, cultural barriers, other issues going on. That's important. Because oh I don't understand this person it's because they're culture. It's the empathic way of you know approaching and the positive regard. That's what we are all trained to have.

It is hard to do it all the time in your seeing like about 25 patients for the morning. It's having that positive regards towards your, that the person that you're dealing with. So not looking through a lens as a generalist. But giving that little bit of extra care towards that person if you feel that this person is struggling to express themselves.

THE ROLE OF THE COMMUNITY IN CELEBRATING DIVERSITY.

If you are from an ethnic minority background and you are in the LGBT community; there are certain services that you need and if you're worried about being judged, you at the end of the day that's going to suffer and not receive the service that you're supposed to receive. I will share some advice struggling to get the right help for their situation.

I think particularly like things like domestic violence, (LGBTQ). They are quite strong issues within the BME communities. Highly controversial and can be extremely difficult to tap in any sort of services. Even the most educated person, sometimes you can have that barrier of not wanting to understand. Because of the cultural layers and I suppose with young people or with the general adults, it's doing your research and finding out where you can get that help. Because these are confidential services. They just need to take that first step. You know test the waters first and do your research and go and find out whether this organization or these professionals can help you or not. Because they are quite strong, very very much tabooed topics. FGM, LGBTQ. Strong topics where many people would not understand. General community, it's difficult even within the general community. It's even more difficult within the BME community.

MY FAVOURITE THINGS ABOUT DIVERSITY

I'm not a big foodie. Nonetheless, I like different types of food. I don't eat a lot. However, I like travel. I love to learn about cultures. I love to learn about human minds. I love travelling. That is something I would love to do more when I get a chance.

Sometimes you get tied up with you know parental responsibilities, work and all sorts of other things. love to travel a bit more. I love to learn about cultures, people, how the human psyche works. I like simple things in life. It doesn't take a lot for me to make myself happy. Little things, friendships, meaningful relationships you know with friends or family or anyone else, meaningful relationships are important.

Diversity brings so much colour into your life. You are not only inside of a vessel. I suppose diversity is being cohesive in a community. Migration is you're migrating from one country to the other country and then starting your life in that new environment, new culture, and new country. But diversity is blending in with different cultures religions and ethnicities

> *"Be whoever you want to be regardless of your race,*
> *educational attainment or where you find*
> *yourself in the world."*
> *- Amina Chitembo*

Bernadetta Omondi

Bernadetta is a Kenyan born British Professional with a teaching background and works in the Public Sector as a Community Connector. She is one of the very few African trained English teachers in the UK. She is the 2018 President of the Peterborough Association of the National Association of Schoolmasters Union of Women Teachers (NASUWT) and sits on the National Disabled Members Advisory Committee.

She was awarded the 2016 Peterborough Civic Award of Community Involvement. She is the chair of the Black History Month Committee Peterborough, and also chairs the Peterborough Community Group Forum, and the Kenya Community Association of Peterborough. Her work centres around reducing systemic barriers to access to services for underserved communities and those with disabilities. Her friends and family know her as Sherrie Anyango.

Area of Expertise:

Raising awareness on Equality, Diversity, and meaningful social mixing.

Raising Awareness of Health Issues including Cancer, Mental Health, and Disability.

Contact Details

bernie@bhmpeterborough.org

https://www.facebook.com/sherrie.anyango

Your Story, My Story, Our History

By Bernadetta Omondi

*"I'm not an exotic fruit. I am an exotic fist to challenge
any exclusion in the community."*

MY MIGRATION STORY: BACKGROUND

As a community champion, I aim to see equality for all. I was born in Kenya. I lived in Nairobi until I migrated to the UK in 2001.

I used to travel to the UK as a tourist. It was on one of my visits that I learnt that the UK had a shortage of teachers. I applied for a job, and I was lucky to get it. I had to go back to Kenya to process my paperwork and come back as a teacher on a work permit. In Kenya, I had taught in secondary schools, both at provincial and national level. I did this for eleven years.

It was not an easy decision to leave my children behind at that young age. I have four children, two adopted, and two of them biological.

Moving to the UK was a start of a new beginning in my career and life in general. I was ready to face the challenge. As soon as I landed in Heathrow, I noted the difference as I was welcomed to chilly weather with the wind whistling and pushing me back with force. At one point I thought that the strong gales were evil force and I started praying asking God for protection.

Before I knew it, February came with heavy snow. I went out of the house to try and touch the snowflakes. Nobody told me that the snow that had settled on the ground was slippery. I landed on the ground with a thud, quickly trying to stand but found myself rolling on the snow instead. The excitement of experiencing the snow became a painful experience.

The word **'difference'** started showcasing in my daily life. I noted the difference in how people walked very first and everyone to themselves. Nobody greeted me as I tried hard to smile at strangers. I was used to a culture where when you got eye contact even with a stranger you would say hello to them. The difference in the way people spoke. I struggled at times to understand the various accents of English people that I met.

The difference in weather, the culture, the clothing, and difference in localities, the difference in the transport system, the buildings, difference in food, the difference between people. I can continue talking of 'differences' as every move I made; I came across something that different from what I knew.

How important does this word have in my life?

1. Adapt: find ways to adapt, as the saying goes, when you go to Rome do as the Romans do. The same way you cannot go to someone's home and expect them to change to suit you. You have to try and learn as many of their ways of living as possible.
2. Equip yourself with the language in order to communicate especially the local dialects, so that you are able to understand and integrate. For example, the cockney way of Londoners or Newcastle Geordie they are quite different, and you might struggle.
3. Ask questions and learn to make friends. Be active in initiating the friendships especially in schools and religious places.

MY TAKE ON DIVERSITY

When I first taught about Diversity to my students. I got a variety of answers.

"Diversity is the dance group in London! Oh no! The dance groups."

I answered, "yes, that's one of them." Anything else you want to tell me?'

Well, I will use the 'Diversity Dance group' then, as an example. Diversity is a UK street dance troupe based in London. I know you can take it as a joke. However, I want to use it because to me Diversity is our difference. Take the dance group; the members are all different.

I used the group as an example where they were different because they came from different backgrounds; race, gender, age, academic levels and even in height. I believe that is why they called

themselves diversity. I remember when I first started teaching Diversity in schools. It was easy for my students to comprehend what Diversity meant from using the example of the Diversity dance group. For me, diversity is our difference. It's imperative for us to recognise our difference in a positive way. Diversity is evident in our communities. For us to live together in harmony, we have to know these differences or understand our differences to accept each other.

Our difference is our strength, wealth, knowledge which when used correctly.

It promotes love, respect, support, confidence and high self-esteem. It can lead to people learning from each other as we are all teachers, we all can learn from each other.

Acceptance and a sense of belonging can help people to integrate into the society; which will ultimately contribute to many of the government initiatives aiming to help diverse communities to be inclusive with each other.

The acceptance will seek to stop wrong perceptions, concepts, prejudice, stereotyping so that we do not ignore talents because of our ignorance. We need to embrace our differences and practise equality within the community. Individual bias has created hatred which has led to an increase in hate crimes and hate incidents. Recently media has shown the difference in Gender pay gap, the disparity of black and ethnic minority in managerial jobs, low numbers of admission of black students in top universities and low attainment grades in education from low-income families.

There is a celebration of Diversity in Britain; however, we all need to work harder at being inclusive. Britain has been a multicultural society for many years nonetheless Britain is still struggling in this century to be inclusive. It seems as though we have not learnt anything from the past on diversity, and therefore, it will never change unless there is a change of perception and behaviour.

We live in a diverse society, but we do not live in an inclusive society. We all need to take responsibility to continue creating awareness of diversity and integration to have a cohesive community. There is a lot of work to be done by ALL to learn about one another. To accept difference, one has to be open and willing to learn. Once you know the difference and you know difference exists, then you will accept difference. Change your mandate on inclusion, diversity will always exist, and inclusion is what we need to work on. We are all One Universal Consciousness, where is the difference between us?

People should not look at our differences and be bias to others.

Diversity is something I saw even in my country of origin. Gender problems have always been prominent even in my country of origin. There are some communities in Kenya that did not see the need to educate a girl child. Boys were the ones who were given education by their parents. Poor families paid school fees for the boys to be educated while girls were quickly married off at a younger age. In some families where both husband and wife worked, the wife would still come home and embark on household chores while the husband sat and watched television.

The wife would still be expected to cook for the husband even after a busy day at work. The men's perception was 'a woman's place is the kitchen'.

There were some occupations which were mainly for men, and it was odd for women even to try. I am happy that women have voiced their opinion and have tried to change the perception. There are now women engineers and in other male-dominated careers. I'm delighted to see women pilots in Kenya flying long haul flights. It does not matter which group you belong to;

you can change the perception by taking responsibility to make a difference.

There were many differences in Africa that were embedded in culture and therefore, nobody would even question it. There were certain roles that were for men and certain chores were for women. It was normal for a woman to stay at home and do the house chores while the man became the main breadwinner.

Roles were divided, and the elders had a final say on most decisions for particular clans or tribes. This in the eyes of many implied that our difference was part of what was accepted by the whole community. Although there were many disparities, individuals accepted them to be part of the norms. This had its disadvantages too because it still led to isolation or fear.

In Kenya, as I was growing up, nobody would disclose if they were in a Lesbian Gay Bisexual Transgender (LGBT) group. They would be killed or cursed by the community. This still shows that it is not only in the UK that we are struggling with inclusiveness. Inclusion should be in every community. I will take my community to mean where I live. That is why in this chapter I will talk about how I see Diversity in the UK.

In the Western world especially here in the UK, the differences are something that people view, so much because of the way many indigenous populations have behaved towards diversity. They seem to have based their dislike on immigration issues in Britain. Some people seem to link Diversity the negative view of immigration. I believe this has made many hate crimes on the race to be more highlighted than other groups.

The prejudice is visible in employment where an ethnicity, gender, age, social status, religion disability and sexual orientation can be used to deter someone's professional development. There are many people with high qualification who are in low paying jobs because their difference they cannot be given the opportunity to show their talents in various roles.

All of these can lead to bullying, hate crimes, hate incidents, exploitation, modern slavery, segregation, to mention a few. We should not have a society where others feel superior; others feel inferior. It is worrying that superiority complex and inferiority complex are significant things in the community. We need to change the narrative by continuing to celebrate diversity

DIVERSITY AND INCLUSION AT WORK AND IN SOCIAL LIFE

The feeling of exclusion or discrimination is something that I've experienced in different ways. There were times when I have felt that in some ways because of being a woman, was less regarded at my workplace. My race not to mention, I am a black woman. Was this a problem for some ignorant people? I would be sitting somewhere, and I'm disregarded and not included in discussions during meetings. I also have a disability.

I gave these ignorant people what they wanted. I call it three in one, I carried them all. I had to work twice as much to make sure I was heard even in a meeting. I resorted to being rude as they call it, interrupt someone until I am left to give my opinion. They later found out that I could provide valid points that would help the department.

Another thing that helped me is that my examination results spoke for itself and the students appreciated what I did with them. This negative treatment impacted on my health and mental well-being. I lost my confidence and my self-esteem and had to be off work for a long time. I would go to some places, and I would be treated differently to an extent where someone would speak to me in English pronouncing words slowly while shouting as if I could not understand them. I started to feel uncomfortable, and it made

me think about why I always had to work harder to prove myself to other people because of my gender, disability or my race.

It was the beginning of me to start to promote diversity. In my teaching career in this country, I was not in a very diverse setting. It had its advantages and its disadvantages.

The students who were predominantly white always wanted to know more about my culture and heritage which I shared with them especially, in my Drama lessons and tutorials.

The students always came to me when I wore African attires; they wanted to learn more about the fabrics and food. It's not only that the difference in the social status, like I, would see during the tutorial. There was a difference between the students who came from social housing and the ones who came from well-off families. I noticed even their manners when they spoke to each other. There were certain places where some of the students from the white community would say they could not go to because it looks 'foreign'. When I asked them, they told me there were many people from Black, Asian, and Minority Ethnic (BAME). It was shocking when students identified themselves with Postcodes and said how they would not mix with certain people from some areas. Peterborough has become a multicultural place rich in culture and Heritage from different communities. Personally, it is a good thing, but others might see it differently. Our differences could be our strength, and our differences could be our failure too. In true form of the title of this book - we all have stories, 'Your story, my story, can be 'our story', our History.

I will conclude by saying, "see the person; not their Disability, Age, Gender, Race, Social Status, Sex Orientation or Religion.

MY WORK LIFE

My first posting as a teacher in the UK was in London. It was tough for me especially, culture shock on the difference in student's behaviour from what I had seen in all my years of teaching in Kenya.

I couldn't believe that students would swear in class, students would have more power than the teacher. There were moments when I felt like I was 'babysitting' and managing the students' behaviour than teaching. I had to be continually thinking of the Health of the safety of my students because of the actions of some a few students.

One day a student sent chills in my spine when they wanted to jump off the window from the first floor. The student just wanted to show off and also seek attention. I was puzzled and quickly asked for help as part of the Behaviour Management. When the senior teacher came, the student started swearing and refused to calm down. "Suddenly I realised I was not the only target for this kind of behaviour." Even the senior teacher who was not a black woman was also a target. It was something I struggled with it because it had a detrimental effect on the other students who wanted to learn.

The constant disruption in class impacted on my mental well-being. I started to fear to go to school thinking that a student might get hurt in my class. These behaviours resorted to lots of paperwork and detention that I hardly had time even to eat while in school. I couldn't believe that I had to be thinking of managing the behaviour of students throughout during the school time. I did not have time to reflect on my teaching if I ever I managed to do so. All my lessons were difficult; they made me question myself and comparing my teaching experience in Kenya and the UK.

I started having nightmares, and I wasn't having enough sleep. I decided that it would be best if I resigned and I went to go back to Africa.

While I was waiting to relocate back to Africa, I came to visit a friend in Peterborough. I started to talk to my inner-self and remembered that I am not a quitter. The new environment was different, a lot calmer. I remembered my young days in primary when we would sing the mantra;

"forward ever backwards never."

In the week when I stayed in Peterborough, constant thoughts of my direction gave me throbbing headaches. I woke up one day, and it was like my late dad was talking to me. He always encouraged me to do my best and not to give up even when the going is tough.

Mmmmmhhh! I pondered on my life. I fear failure, and for a moment I gasped, there is no turning back. I then remembered the famous saying.'

"Nothing beats a failure but a try".

In my dad's vocabulary, there was no word 'I can't', so I was going to try teaching again. I started applying for teaching jobs and got a post with an Agency as a Supply teacher. When God has opened the door, nobody can close it. Within a month I was called for an interview through my Agency to a Secondary School.

I was successful and got the post as a Drama Teacher, and the school renewed my work Permit. The contract went beyond the initial agreement. While in that school I started looking for a permanent post. I taught since until February 2017 when I had to change my job due to health reasons. Here again found different responses from both students and teachers.

In Kenya when a teacher walked into class the first is respect not only because they're a teacher but because they are an adult. It did not matter who walked in class as long as they were an adult. The students respected the school staff, property and the environment. It meant, no swearing or breaking things, for example, breaking pens and pencil to throw at other students.

The appropriate language was used all times in the presence of a teacher. Parents evening was to discuss a student's progress and behaviour but not to be used by the parent to question my teaching as they did in two schools. At one point, my accent became an issue for some people. It did not matter how good I was at my work. I was a foreigner with an accent. I had taught UK citizens from different parts of the UK who had strong accents, but they were accepted because they were from within the UK.

The experiences made me feel that I wasn't valued at all, even with the parents and at times as students would ask silly questions that would go back to my race. As a grown-up, I was expected to cope with these issues. I lived in fear that if I raised the issues; I would lose my job. There was no one to share my problems with.

I suffered in silence and only prayed to God for the situation to change.

"That which does not kill us makes us stronger."
- Friedrich Nietzsche

These experiences made me a stronger person than I thought. I started going to union meetings and conferences. I found out that I was not the only black woman with a disability and who experienced frequent attacks.

My eye opened, and I became hungry to get more knowledge on how to be assertive. I stood up to these bullies and accepted to be elected a union Representative to be a voice of the voiceless. I became fearless and ready to face any bully. I realised the passion I had to help others, and I became David, prepared to face any Goliath. I was ready to pounce at anybody who I felt had threatening behaviours in myself or my colleges because of their difference in any of the protected characters. I started inspiring others to stand up and face these ignorant, selfish people.

I recruited many to the union which later got support, not only for their profession but also for their Health and Mental Wellbeing. There was no stopping me, and I was on a mission to encourage not only women but anyone regardless of their difference who was facing discrimination because of who they were.

"It took me quite a long time to develop a voice, and now that I have it, I am not going to be silent."
- Madeleine Albright

LESSONS FOR NEW ARRIVALS

I want to take you through the experience I had myself when I moved in Peterborough. I use Peterborough because that's where I have lived more than anywhere else in the UK.

When I moved to my own house after getting the job contract I found there were five bins in the following colours; black, brown, green and then two grey ones.

It took me a while before I could master which rubbish goes into which colour bin. One day, I put textile in the green bin. That bin was not emptied by the Council that day. I called the Council to check why my bin was not collected. The Council said that it was because my bin was contaminated.

The word 'contamination' made me think that my bin had bacteria or virus. I just did not know that was the word they used when a wrong thing was put in the wrong bin.

Nobody showed me where the important amenities were like **doctors' surgery,** the banks, libraries and how to use public transport (weekly bus pass).

I really struggled when settling in, so I took it upon myself to help new arrivals that I came across. It was weird, anytime I saw a black person, I would stop them and introduce myself. I even gave them my contact details in case they wanted help.

Believe it or not, through that I started connecting with many people. I got invited to their social events and got to know many families. My network grew, and I joined many community groups in most of the activities around the city. These connections helped me to signpost newcomers to relevant community groups of their origin.

We noted that most communities had same needs and so it would help to join our resources. These groups decided to revive a community forum that was at a verge of collapsing. And share whatever we had. I was hungry to be a voice of the voiceless and did not want anyone to have an experience that I had. Nine different community groups joined together to continue with The Peterborough Community Group Forum (PCGF) relaunched in 2011.

I was surprised to be nominated to be the Chairperson. I accepted the post not knowing that PGCF would attract many community groups from black and other ethnic minorities. By 2013 I was chairing monthly twenty-two community groups and helped them by linking them with different service providers. This became a platform for guest speakers to come and give information to the community leaders and also community groups got more information of the services they needed.

A couple few tips for you:

Tip one: You can make a difference regardless of who you are and where you come from. You do not have to wait for someone else to change what is not going right for you or your community.

Tip two: Remember, we are all citizen of the world. You can work with any human being without looking at their difference but accept them the way they are. Language should not be a barrier. There are other forms of communication. People who struggled to speak English language have can be encouraged to use even one word and mix it with other body language to communicate.

Many people who thought they had poor English managed to feel included by performing in the events by showcasing their food, music, arts and crafts. By building their confidence to participate PCGF was able to signpost them with colleges and other organisation that run ESOL classes.

POSITIVE RESULTS OF CELEBRATING DIVERSITY

I remember that vividly in 2015 a few of us from the Peterborough Community Group Forum (PCGF) decided to have a Multi-Cultural event at the centre of the town to celebrate Diversity. The was an opportunity to show that although we had different cultures, there are still things that brought people together. We used music and food to be the main things, although we also had a stall that had arts and crafts. This event was successful, and I think it inspired us to continue to want to showcase our rich culture and heritage in the middle of town. How beautiful it was to have the of Peterborough having different community groups Lithuanian folk dance, Polish dance group, Irish Band, Black Rapper, Portuguese and East Timorese, Asians all came together to celebrate their diverse talents. It was a powerful event showing we are stronger by acknowledging our difference. Accepting that we all have skills and it doesn't matter whether we have language barrier we can still overcome it and use other forms of communication. Tolerance and respect are critical because we all learn differently at our own pace. The young people were given their slots; they performed a street dance. We had disabled people just coming to watch and joined in the dancing. It was just beautiful seeing everyone enjoying themselves. I remember a young girl with hearing impairment performing to the audience by playing an instrument. I've never forgotten this that there was a girl with death and she was there playing an instrument. We need to celebrate Diversity in any form as we are stronger together in building ourselves and the community. We don't only celebrate the racial differences, but the difference in other protected areas as well.

I have since organised various events at Cathedral Square supported by Peterborough City Council which promote social mixing.

In these events, I have engaged with different organisations to create awareness of Hate Crime, Modern Slavery, Mental Health, Cancer and celebrating diversity as part of Black History Month.

I still put my teaching role as part-time after I embarked started working as a Community Connector in 2017. The is a job I had done for twelve years on a voluntary basis is now earning me a salary. I'm proud to have been a community champion as one who wants to promote Diversity in the City. I want people to know that our difference is our strength. I still go to schools to link inspirational speakers to talk about diversity which at that young age can lead to Bullying. The information will continue to equip students with knowledge based on our differences. For Example, Refugees, Asylum seekers and economic immigrants. I went with the British Red Cross to link then with schools to explain how they support Refugees. To explain why people, migrate to different countries and how as Human Beings they can be supported welcomed in the country. I was one of the people in Peterborough who campaigned for the Council to accept Syrian refugees in Peterborough. I was not a Council employee at that time but represented Peterborough Community Group Forum. The panel met at

Peterborough Asylum & Refugee Community Association (PARCA) in Unity Hall is where the committee met for months to pursue the settlement of the Syrians in Peterborough. I was in that panel too. It is a great joy to Syrian families settling in Peterborough, there children attending schools and majority working hard to learn English so that they can integrate freely in the community.

The CEO PARCA Mr Moez Nathu has worked to lead an organisation that supports Refugees in the City. He is a role model to many refugees in the city to be empowered to a level to want to help others to settle and achieve to their potential. He also struggled with the English language as he spoke fluent French, Kiswahili and Lingala. Moez can now read and write in English and has ESOL projects in his organisation to help other refugees and asylum seekers. I supported this organisation by editing their posters and letters before they could be sent to clients from 2004. This is now an established organisation with employed administrators.

They do many events and projects that promote Integration and Diversity.

The Differences Between Diversity and Inclusion are;

Diversity is our difference, which has its advantages and disadvantages. Everyone has to take responsibility to fit in and the others to accept and respect people around them. To promote Diversity, we have to make sure we have the right proportion of what we are doing. There has to be equality for all so that there is no division where some people are superior and others feeling inferior. I like examples; I will use 'baking a cake. For a cake to rise and be tasty, the baker must make sure that they get the right measurement for each ingredient. The baker has to mix the dough well mixing evenly every element. If you don't measure correctly, then your cake will be flat or break into pieces. Baking a cake is like baking a cake because in Diversity people need to interact well with each other with mutual respect.

Your difference should not be a hindrance to engagement with people. I don't like using the word 'tolerance' because it shows there is already something wrong. Instead, I will use the word 'acceptance'. It should be a matter of everybody taking responsibility and trying to work together. The more you engage, the more you will be able to understand each other regardless of your difference. After knowing that someone does not mean harm to you, you need to accommodate their views and try and understand their background.

Meaningful social mixing is critical for community members, not to be just a one-off engagement.

Mixing freely to understand each other regardless of people's difference in age, differences in gender, differences in social status, differences in religion, differences in sexual orientation, is what I call inclusion. My fingers are not the same but on the same body. Imagine one of my fingers is injured; I believe the whole palm will be affected. I will struggle to do other things. They all move together to make that positive outcome of anything you want to do. Likewise, everybody as mentioned in the groups above, the moment one feels excluded from the function of the community they will be affected. For the hands to function the fingers correctly, have to be able to have full movement and grip of things. Any mobility problem of these fingers can affect the whole-body function.

In my opinion, therefore, Inclusion is when all people get an equal chance to participate in any activity as part of the wider community. Everybody needed to be treated the same and included regardless of their difference. We should consider everyone's needs when we make plans. By giving everyone a chance to participate in any decision or actions make them have a sense of belonging and a boost to their self-esteem. Through participation and the feeling of acceptance, we can all make individuals to show their skills and talents regardless of our difference.

Diversity is our difference; our difference should not be a hindrance to our progress in the society. Just like in teaching, there has to be differentiation to meet everyone's needs hence, inclusion.

I am also going to add what I see as meaningful social mixing. Social meaning to me is where you mix with people socially. It could be in different groups. You're mixing for a purpose. Community members should use open common spaces to engage with others even if it is small scale. You can meet a place like the parks and have community activities like games or picnic. We have to be proactive and find ways of having sustainable social mixing for the community.

Meaningful social mixing will only occur if the activities are maintained and are aimed for a purpose so that it is not just for ticking boxes. People can meet in various activities at events. Let organisations go to the community to make it accessible to all community members rather than look for venues that are far from the targeted groups. The connections made should help in building a positive relationship, change of behaviour and perceptions of our difference. We are rich in culture and talents, let us use these opportunities to learn from each other. Let us share our knowledge with the younger generations who are the future leaders of tomorrow so that we do not lose our culture and heritage.

Sharing leads to the positive outcome of the change of behaviour. Social mixing can be a tool to empower other if promoted well in the community with common interest.

I met a good friend from community meetings who has shared most of her artworks in various events in the city of Peterborough and beyond. At almost 80 years old, Morgan Fitzsimons still does volunteer work to support students in schools through creative Arts. In her workshop, you can see the inter-generational engagement. Morgan, a white female with a disability has engaged with children during Black History month colouring African colouring book that she produced. Through numerous meetings, we built the relationship, and Morgan played a significant part in my daughter's wedding.

She designed the invitation cards by drawing my daughter's portrait and that of her husband's. Many people could not believe that she could create such a good card because of her age.

The lesson here is that we should not go with people's perceptions to judge others. Our prejudice towards others comes from our opinions. See the person and not age. Morgan is an International winning Author -Artist who was a teacher. Her age and disability have not stopped her from supporting many community groups and organisations with her skills. To me, that is meaningful social mixing where we learn from each and impact on other people's lives.

Many young people and community members have benefitted from engaging with Morgan as she is a powerhouse of knowledge and goes to many workshops as a speaker/ artist. This scenario is an excellent example of meaningful social mixing across generations, age, race, educational backgrounds and cultures.

FINAL WORD

Our differences are our strengths. We need to respect each other and not have wrong perceptions about others irrespective of their differences. We need to empower community members to accept each other. We all need to take responsibility to make sure we do not isolate anybody because they are different. Everyone needs to try to play a positive role to promote social mixing to make Britain an inclusive place. Britain is diverse, but not yet as inclusive as it could be. If in 1950's people spoke of the need of people in Britain to be inclusive, it is a shame that even now we are still talking of inclusion. Everybody should have a sense of belonging within the community. The other thing is security; you can only feel safe if you make the environment safe. The way you engage with others matters. Respect people around you although they might be different. Equip yourself with the tools to enhance communication. Learn the language to make you confident. Do not be afraid to ask for help and also engage in community initiatives to have friends. Isolation leads to loneliness which can cause mental health issues.

My Biggest Diversity Wish for the World

"One love."

I wish I could sing. 'We are the world' by USA Africa. I wish people would embrace our difference and live in harmony. Bob Marley summed it up by singing 'One Love. Let's love one another in the community. Unity is essential; together we can change the world. Let us all join hands together and teach our youth the need for togetherness. Empower them

This is my story, my understanding of diversity and inclusion. What's your story? Will it be our history?

Charity Ngugi-Latz

Education: Studied at the Kenya High School and the University of Nairobi. Graduated with a Bachelor of Arts Honours degree in Literature.

Occupation: Author, Blogger, Speaker and part-time research and news editor at Sonnenblumen Community Development group e.V an international NGO. Active voluntary worker with the Afro migratory groups in Köln

Hobbies: Active member- FremdWörte a Writer, Authors and Translators group. Member: Der Künste der welt and LiteraturHaus Köln and Gemeinde Christi Köln.

Published co-authored book: The Perfect Migrant" "Crossing Borders in Search of dignity." and Celebrating Diversity "The Trail-Blazers of Universal inclusion".

Method of working: Digital storytelling, and oral literature "Spoken Word"

Online articles about Migration, Universal inclusion and Domestic Violence.

Online and offline debates on the series: The Trail-Blazers Episodes touching on lifestyles, thoughts, education, and climate change.

Contacts.

https://www.universal-inclusion.org

Email: wakamauson12@gmail.com

cwlatz@yahoo.de

Telephone: +4917684207246 /+491786378648 / +254720547201 / fax+4922158871089

Trailblazers of Universal Inclusion

Charity Ngugi-Latz

INTRODUCTION

I was born in Kenya a former British colony, four years before it gained its independence on 12th December 1963. There were three of us, a sister who lives in Germany and my last-born brother who passed away in 2002 from colon cancer. We were brought up by my mother, the late Grace Nduta Gathea who was a senior Air hostess with Kenya Airways formerly East African Airways. We lived in a mortgaged house in Nairobi, Harambee Estate in a middle-class neighbourhood. This is where I spent my teenage and adult years. It was a community of mixed tribes. The language of our residential community was inter-mixed English and Swahili although at home my mother spoke to us in Gikuyu. I now fully appreciate this as I have learnt how important it is to maintain one's cultural heritage and language. I also attended a girls-only boarding school, in Nairobi the capital city, and it was an inter-mix of diverse races of Africans, Indians and Europeans.

The school had a strict The Queen of England educational system. We had foreign diverse extra-curricular activities of English sports; such as tambourine, tennis and hockey, plus a very English diet and very strict English table manners. Although the school's educational curriculum in Kenya is designed along the England standards, Kenya High School where I did both my high school and higher school-form five and six levels was one of the few outstanding schools with a very extra-Europeanised culture. The school fees were also very high, and I thank my late mother for all her sacrifices. I never missed school due to lack of fees charges even once. My brother and sister also attended similar grade schools: The Upper Hill secondary for boys and State House girls' high school respectively. I, therefore, had a very diverse, well-founded educational and disciplined background.

The school system did not discriminate along race or social status, and we were all handled equally. Interesting enough l came to learn and experience racism in my later years after l migrated to Europe. But despite all that, l chose to learn and try to understand what our belief differences were and to avoid unnecessary conflicts based on ignorance.

Celebrating diversity is all about dignity and universal inclusion and understanding that we are all valuable and can be leaders in our diverse societies.

My father was born in 1935, and he studied at the University of Nairobi and for six months in Scotland in the discipline of Arts and Crafts. He worked as a senior advisor of schools under the Ministry of education, Department of Arts. I once discussed with my father about his experiences in Scotland, and he only had good memories about it. He told me that the education especially in the field of Art in Edinburg was the best in the 1960's.He, however, admitted that there was minimum integration with the Europeans after classes. He said that people stuck to their own race groups even in the hostel sections but there was no direct violence or intimidation. My father being a very private person and very passionate with his Art work probably was not bothered by the isolation.

A friend once asked me how it was growing up so soon after independence in Kenya. The truth is that I never directly experienced the pains of colonialism. I grew up in a home and area where education was very valued and prioritised. Every single area we lived in was structured with identical housing similar to housing in England, what we called Estates.

Ours were Madaraka Estate with my dad for three years and New Ngara Flats and Harambee Estate with my late mum. They were designed by the City Council of Nairobi with outside playing ground facilities and City council health centres. In both areas, it was the same middle -class families.

Kenya after 1963 transited very smoothly and was very stable under its First president the late Jomo Kenyatta. We did not experience any kind of severe political or social discrimination. Comparatively, many said that we were under a neo-colonial rule. How true that is not the discussion of this chapter.

What l perceived in my thoughts was peace and love growing up in an environment of harmony among different tribes. I think my late mother, for she protected and provided for us adequately; so we never lacked. It was also common for all parents to protect not only their children but the neighbour's children. I thank my mother for showing us how to be loving and social as was her personality. I am also grateful to her for giving me a character that does not know what it is to look down upon others and a spirit that she demonstrated of sharing and serving.

My father after his retirement worked from home in Batik making until two years ago when he started suffering from dementia and diabetes. However, I continue to help him in the sales of most of his remaining Batik artworks; cards, wall hangings, bags and calendars during the festive periods of Christmas and Easter.

My Parent's Divorce and How My Life Changed

"The unexamined life is not worth living."
-Socrates

My parents divorced when I was about five years. My younger sister and I lived with my father for 2 years or less; I really do not know because that part of my life is somehow buried due the traumatic experiences we had of child abuse labour and physical, sexual from my aunt, while my late brother resided with my mother.

However, after my mum learnt of these incidents and especially since there was no intervention from my father who was aloof and absents my mother took over custody of all three of us until her passing away in November 1982. We had no contact with my father who chose to neglect us.

I lived in Kenya until the age of thirty-seven, when I migrated to Germany to marry my late husband, Helmut Latz. After graduating, I worked for a parastatal insurance company as a Life insurance underwriter where I had the experience of working in an accounting field other than Literature.

In my position, I was in charge of handling client's applications for policy loans and dealing with insurance death payments to the policyholders next of kin. The lessons I learnt in this position was how to handle sensitive cases especially when dealing with death payments to the next of kin.

Due to the diversity of cultures in relation to death, one must be very careful because in most African traditions it is a taboo to talk about death. Also, being a young woman in a senior position some men and even women next of kin did not think I could handle their death claims. But with time I learnt a lot on how to be more empathic as well as professional and to respect the cultural structures of the African community. As the years went by Kenya started to grow to a stage where women were being accepted as equal in office.

However, in my older years my father and I have re-established a close relationship. Because of his old age and dementia, he has left me with some valuable artwork which I appreciate him for. During my travels l try to sell it in order to pay for his maintain the farm and house l built for us on our family land. In the art-work enclosed below, I would have loved to know more about his mind set in this piece.

When l view it, I see a lot of details depicting a celebration of Diversity. The colourful man in traditional attire dancing and

drumming. Observe the steps, sandals and colours. If you are into Art, I will let you build your own thoughts dear reader on this wonderful piece.

DIVERSITY MEANS UNIVERSAL INCLUSION

This other Artwork also portrays a woman at the marketplace and men negotiating the price of the huge baskets or could be gourds. What is important is that it pot rays and celebrates the diversity of working spaces and equality. With my experiences, I then needed

to start positioning all this knowledge that I have gained, and I started to find a way off as to what and how I could share my message to the world in my new found calling. I picked on "Universal Inclusion" as my business brand name.

It was through brainstorming with my coach and mentor; Amina Chitembo who is a UK based Zambian author, speaker trainer and coach. She is also a publisher who helped me to write and publish my first co-authored published work: "The Perfect Migrant". She continues to encourage me to write helping me to get over my fears and procrastinating through coaching mentorship. The brand name set off a new train of thoughts, with a lot of clarity. It helped define who I was and what I stood for; social activism, dignity inclusion, equality and transparency, when combined are my new-found purpose. Universal inclusion to me means recognising individual differences. It means embracing a diverse environment in all its wholeness as a planet. Universal inclusion is in one word celebrating diversity.

> *"We are all imperfectly perfect."*
> *– Amina Chitembo*

In in the chapter I wrote in the book 'The Perfect Migrant' I shared my struggles in the second chapter 'Across Borders in Search of Dignity'. The book is available on Amazon, or you can contact me directly for a signed copy. My past is not perfect. I struggled with alcohol issues, ill health, self-esteem and other life journey plights like financial loss and eventually, I am rising day by day into a life of meaning and purpose. I want to just reference it to paint a picture for you about where I am coming from.

After the death of my husband Helmut, I started on a self-therapy journey at times travelling to the coastal area of Mombasa on my own for not less than a month. I love the ocean, and the people there are very warm, and it is a completely different environment from Nairobi due to its weather, it very relaxed, welcoming people and the tourism atmosphere. I went through many phases of committed church-going and initiated a creativity club for children in Gemeinde Christi Cologne (Church of Christ).In the church is where l started having my first healthy personal relationships almost like family, with native Germans and other foreigners from all over the world.l felt loved and assured that my life was worthy, and l could be of value to so many people.l also spent a lot of my free time online researching on spirituality,doing free writing courses and seeking to find my purpose, knowing I needed help and stability.

One of the significant things that happened is that l just had this great awakening in my heart especially when the news was perpetually flooded with the influx of immigrants and a lot of them dying at seas, deserts and refugee camps to be in one way or another involved.

I suddenly realised that I was very fortunate in that I was free and independent, a permanent resident in Germany and my children were now financially stable, educated and grown-ups with the youngest now over 20 years old.

I decided to play a more active role and voice the plight of these underprivileged, homeless, through taking small concrete steps. I decided to turn my life and start interacting with positive and uplifting people. I now appreciate people as I get to interact with diverse people from all walks of life, ages, gender and nationalities. They have helped me regain my self-confidence and l realise just how many wonderful people are walking on this planet. It has opened my eyes to discover that one small concrete initiative in collaborative work can go a long way to rebuilding the destroyed structures in our cities and even bring global awareness and universal peace.

All this is possible because of the diversity that we share. Each of these people has in their own way a diverse set of backgrounds, skills and experiences. They have included me and shared their knowledge with me. That is Universal Inclusion at play.

Without much thought I have recovered and have uncovered I have been in my own way sharing the light and been a trailblazer of my destiny. Through endless free time research, and my voluntary duties at the refugee halls of residence and /or by joining them where they relax, I have gathered a lifetime of information that has left me grateful to the Most High, Supreme, Divine God. I believe in the freedom of worship, and I respect that everyone has a right to be affiliated to The Spirit of their heart, be it yoga, singing, dancing, praying, meditating or fasting. It is right that each seeks to receive what they want and need and that everyone respects others individual space and violates no one's dignity. This is a universal inclusion motto.

Professional and personal development have been key to my appreciation of Diversity. I love reading, I have more than 300 books in my library, and I read at least a minimum of a new book every week as the way to learn. I am enrolled in online and offline courses to be better at my narrative style of writing and filming. I also join other artists and writers from all walks of life, and I must say that I have encountered acceptance and have not experienced hostility in my journey to self-discovery. A lot of people, in fact, are consciously awakening to the positive effects of cultural interactions.

The Bible says; *"seek and you shall find"*, and *I fully trust that if one gives enough priority to their passion and to learn a new skill, one will* be fulfilled eventually. In Europe, education is available, and in German it is free, and when one is financially disabled, there is sponsorship for all levels of education. Self-development courses are available online and at other platforms. One has to get out of their comfort zones and seek by asking.

Celebrating diversity means asking for help and giving out support in the way of exchanged information and teaching others new skills. The concept of universal inclusion recognises the idea of entitlement and crediting others for a job well done. It is realising that we are entitled to live freely on this globe doing diverse universal things with what we have and what we love doing so long as it is productive and not harmful to either self or others.

The Four things l can teach someone about inclusion in finding themselves are the following.

1. It is paramount to come out of a crowd or group mentality by realising that you are not defined by the colour of your skin, your religious or spiritual affiliation, your gender, your age or any other self-imposed beliefs that have been limiting you from moving forward. What is important is to know that you are first and foremost a child of the Universe entitled fully to be alive on this planet.

2. What I call "self-therapy" is giving yourself "ME-Time" to reflect about you, your daily thoughts, vision and your vision and purpose.Forget and erase from your mind the thought that it is selfish to think about your self. By learning to know about yourself,you will know where you are lacking and seek help and clarity from others who have been on a similar path but have overcome. Through meditation, prayer, or whatever way you choose to speak to your inner person, doors will open and advise, and help will arrive in unexpected ways.

3. Self-development is essential, and ignorance is not an excuse. Go online, to the library, read, listen attend seminars etc. Never stop learning and age is just a number not

a sickness, there continue improving on your skills and talents. Get out of your comfort zone and take small steps to share your knowledge.

4. Love the Lord your God with all your heart, soul, mind and strength and your neighbour as you love yourself.

THE TRAILBLAZER MINDSET

"A Trailblazer is an individual who has taken up the role of being an active participant and NOT just an observer, a bystander or unproductive critic."

WHO IS A TRAILBLAZER?

There a number of definitions of who a trailblazer is. I like to think of it this way; A Trail-Blazer is an individual who has chosen a path of embracing the thought that we are all dignified and that as human beings we are capable of great love and empathy. They also amplify the fact that it is possible to change one's ways and embrace dignity as a lifestyle of reconciliation and peace. This entails being open-minded to the world. Let me kick off this chapter by sharing another one of my dad's art pieces.

When I observe this Batik work I see the celebrity of motherhood and the appreciation of the diversity of cultural clothing or fashion wear, embroidery, healthy love and upbringing of a child. What do you my reader see? I would love to hear your answers on my website blog.

"Who are we and what is our purpose on this planet?".

As a Trailblazer, my main purpose is to serve. However, it can seem overwhelming, due to the strained relationships amongst the human race now more than ever before, surmounted by the escalating climate change and environmental hazards. Peace seems like a far-fetched word when one observes the wars cropping up

all over the world and the migration crisis. The economic gap between the classes of people is widening day by day and poverty is paramount. However, I still believe in the goodness of mankind, and I think we're naturally very precious as human beings because of our unique capacities of communication and high consciousness. What about if we all adopted an attitude of celebrating each other and accepting our universality as one? I have pondered on this and perceived it possible.

At the forefront of my research was my thought that surely, we are not in this world by mistake nor are we a "maybe" kind of people. I knew I had a purpose and I discovered it was a question of **having a positive mindset.** This is a mindset of gratitude and appreciation of what and who you are. We could start by being consciously aware of the free knowledge available in this century all over the world.

We could start by learning about how other people live, how we can make ourselves happy and in turn affect those around us with a positive mindset or attitude. I decided to bring it forward; I set up blogs one is called "AN ENCOUNTER WITH GOD" or AEWGM in short which is part of my greater mission. It was founded in 2012. It was born out of the need to evangelise and enrich the perishing youth with sound-basic life skills. AEWGM is meant to be an inspiration tower and a stream of God's love. Since inception, we have partnered with several community-based organizations with a similar vision and belief in Universal Inclusion.

AEWGM uses art, internet classes, sports, mentorship and counselling to achieve its objective of spreading love and creating more encounters of inclusion across generations. We celebrate each other on a daily basis through sharing and recognition of each person's sacredness as a human being

The other blog I host is "UNMASKED STORIES". which features authentically untold or unheard stories from different people and communities so as to entertain, preserve culture, educate, inspire and advocate for change. I started it around 2017

I continue to interact daily with like-minded people and attend seminars on mindfulness, Empowerment, Non-Violence communication, investment and Startup business growth. It was by sheer coincidence that I picked up this title "Trailblazer" after attending Steve Odhiambo's seminar in Stuttgart.

A positive mindset celebrates people and protects the earthlings from harm. When celebrating our diversity, we acquire a caring consciousness that leads to a clearer mind. We start to explore higher because we discern there is a more and better lifestyle of greatness and excellence. Communication in various circumstances becomes less rigid as we value each other. We can conclude that it is only fair and human to treat others kindly wherever you find yourself at any given waking moment

What has this got to do with celebrating diversity?

How is one expected to react or address the answer?

Celebrating cultural diversity is also another process of learning with curiosity and joy about other people cultures and being polite enough not to be rude or adamantly reject anything outside our comfort zone or familiarity. The fundamental goals of human interactions are to exchange ideas, make dignified conversations and collaborate by working together happily, in harmony. Currently, in Germany especially what l witness in Cologne over the weekends is a lot of interactions of both people of colour and the Europeans and other nationalities. The Germans especially, love learning about the traditional cultures of other people and even the language. In Köln, we have started the Swahili Cultural Club with Wambui Elsen at Sonnenblumen Community Development group an international NGO, and we have many registered foreigners engaged in learning the language and children are the major participants. Notably, Swahili is being proclaimed as the United language of Africa What l have observed with a growing interest of late is a celebration of diversity in the music field of Rap and Reggae in the dance steps and beats. As a descendant of the Agikuyu in Kenya, we are also having festivals in Germany where we showcase our traditional way of celebrating a newborn child and welcoming them into the community in a ceremony known as "Itega". The "Itega" ceremony is an alternative way of introducing to the German natives and other foreign friends our beautiful heritage. In the same manner, we get to celebrate Carnivore in Köln. It is a five-day event full of dancing, fun and fancy, colourful costumes like Halloween in America. During this time people get to be very kind. Passing caravans dish out chocolates, sweets and flowers and Kölch (Köln) music is played loud on the streets, and kölsch beer served on the streets. It is a great way to interact and kill of the stress of the year.

Kenya the Diversity Country

Kenya is in East Africa. It is a country made up of 44 tribes and an even larger significant number of different speaking languages (mother tongues). Each tribe has and maintains its unique cultural structure and a lot of the traditions are still practised to date. Let me give you now a clearer picture as to why I use all my four names. Amongst the Agikuyu, my cultural heritage, the naming of the child and the celebration of the child are significant occasions. The naming follows a traditional, strict order. As the first-born, I was named after my grandmother on my father's side "Charity Wairimu". All the first-born daughters born into the Njai family, my late grandfather's surname are named after my grandmother.In the same manner all first-born sons are named after my grandfather "Stephen Njai."as was the case with my late brother. The second child boy or girl is named after the grandfather or grandmother on the maternal side as is the case of my sister Joyce (Nancy) Nyambura, my lovely late mothers mother. She was also an adorable woman with a very strong personality.

My full names are Charity Wairimu Ngugi Latz. I value all four of my names because they celebrate my experiences as a woman of varied cultures and environments and belonging to two countries: Kenya and German where I reside.

However, the name Charity Wairimu has a special place in my heart because of my grandmother's legendary hospitality and kindness not only to me but the whole community of Muguga and Kahuho my home village in Kenya.My other name "Ngugi" is the last name of my father, James Ngugi Njai. The last name "Latz" is from my late husband, Helmut Latz. After getting acquainted with many Europeans l discovered that they too have a traditional way of giving names. This makes us all universally similar and yet different in many other ways.

My concluding statement is that we must try to treat our living space with dignity, uphold our cultural heritage and give our ample time to making the world a place where nobody is left out in eating the fruits of the land. The earth is big enough to accommodate every single human being and to include every single person in its peace treaties. Let's treat each other with dignity and let's abhor war and discrimination. Let us welcome others into our midst knowing fully that migration is still old as eons and only part of our short-lived journey on earth. After all migration gives us all a chance to get to know each other and erase our insignificant, naivety about the world and what lies beyond our limited knowledge. Let us therefore with one accord continue to celebrate one another in our diversity and worthy life.

Malcim enjoy the journey Roland

Roland Burt

Roland Burt founder of Djibo Art. I can't stay still! I love painting and making things! The brighter and expressive, the better!

I grew up in North Yorkshire as part of a large Caribbean family. My passion for painting on anything - kitchen towels, canvas and wood blossomed from an early age, and as I grew up it became a conduit for life's stresses and challenges. I'd return to my art whenever I found myself needing a sanctuary and a reprieve from pressure, before once again tackling the day.

I've always been a bit of a magpie of cultural influences. I remember being totally fascinated at school by Neolithic cave paintings, Art Deco, West Indian and African art.

My life and work have taken me to France, Canada, Italy, Turkey, Bulgaria to name but a few, and everywhere I found something local to be fascinated by.

Painting has always been the key to who I'm today. Painting for me is storytelling. The story usually takes precedent over shapes and colour. Also, painting is like dreaming – dreaming in a multitude of colours, bright images and perpetual restless movement.

Contact Details:
http://www.djiboart.co.uk/
Email: info@djiboart.co.uk
Facebook: https://www.facebook.com/ArtDjibo/

Diversity in a Child of Yesterday

By Roland Burt

"No spoon in my mouth just a brush."

Well if I said that I am a bit of Mongrel, then people will start laughing. When you say Mongrel, they think poorly of the animal. They think of it as an inferior breed. Believe it or not, I think having a bit of history from different parts of the world actually creates something better and enhances the term Mongrel.

Let me explain you can tell with my accent that I was born here in England obviously North England a little place called Castleford not too far from Leads. So first of all, I am a Yorkshire man. Ok you can stop raising your eyebrows and laughing. My mum is from an island called Dominica, so is Caribbean that's an exotic mix so far. Picture next a French-Canadian father, now you're thinking what else maybe? My great-grandfather on his side was Ghanaian.

So to summarise we have bit of African, a dash of French-Canadian, a strange English accent a beautiful tan from my mum, whom others pay a fortune to attain whilst on holiday.

I have an exotic British Afro French-Canadian Caribbean feel about me hahahaha Something to note; my mum can trace her ancestry back to the original Indians, the Arawaks. They are the original Inhabitants of the Caribbean not as history is written by conquerors that they were from Africa, they are actually South American.

Maybe if we think of the world when it formed all the excitement and the drama of the earth splitting off and the sea formation and the land settling volcanoes with the power and beauty of creation, the perception is that it we started in Africa but what about the possibility that it also started, in another part of the world as the world broke up people travelled towards the new islands that were formed and they travelled to Africa as the African travelled from Africa to the new world.

I used to fantasize about travellers moving from one part of the world to the other and I always dreamt this happened to create such beautiful and diverse peoples on the Islands. Educated people have proven that the peoples on the islands are actually Indians, Proving immigration from different directions potentially. Therefore, I am not just Indian African French or British. I am the sum of many parts made beautiful that is the world. So now you know a little about me, what's your story?

Nature has many different forms, yet we all stem from the same well. My hope is that this is shown in the many stories shown in my paintings.

REPLICATING MY PAINTING IN ART

It's a very broad subject so may I give you couple of instances to how and why I bring my famous traditions my heritage?

So, I am painter by profession, I became professional in 2017 although in reality, I have been painting since the age of four. However, its 2017 that I decided I was going to take such a massive step.

We all have to take that step, we all have to come out from our comfort zone, to take that first step on that ladder, on that path, put our feet in the sea of possibilities. Before that though, I spent the previous year researching and trying to figure out where my place was in life. I don't want to be a poor artist. This was going to be a completely different experience for me. I alone would be the master of my destiny I am not actually interested in the trappings of wealth, but what I am looking for is a rich life that celebrates the best of human nature and experiences, and painting giving rewards for my clothing food and bills.

So the first part of my journey to become a professional began with me standing in the middle of the street with some of my images and I would ask passers by what they thought of each particular style etcetera and from that I would build an understanding that I may have indeed something to offer and then I walked around the different galleries and places and after being rejected by virtually everyone I came to realise that I probably did have something to offer, when one lone voice said *"yes we love your work"*. This was the Visitors Centre where even today they still stock and sell my work. I then decided after some ups and downs shall we say, which I will elaborate later, I would then get the professionals to notice me.

My first exhibition was at a national bank, where again I used the experience as part of my research and had a successful day. I still didn't believe I was going to make a good enough living out of this.

I realized that my father was nearing the end of his journey soon, his illness was now a major concern, and I decided if I wanted to do something with my life for him to be proud of me, even more, it had to be now or never. So, I approached the management of the largest garden centre that I knew at that time and delivered my proposals. I was surprised when they said "OK we like your ideas we shall give it a go. Unfortunately, he did not live long enough to see the launch of my business at that centre; he passed on the day my business went live.

The first person who bought a piece of art work wow! If I told you I was in shock excited and numb someone believed in me and was doing me the honour of hanging it up in their home Wow.

Such a feeling gave me further motivation that I really did have to something to offer the world.

That was June 29th, **last year 2017, it is just over a year that I am in business** and it has snowballed from there really. The ideas I had for the work in charities and schools would now be easier to deliver, as I was able to earn an income to enable me to help others, and that's why for an example I work with three charities. I work with *St Gemmas Hospice in Leeds I work with Circles Network Peterborough* and my other Charity work is around community centres and special needs schools, all funded from the main business. I really do enjoy creating and storytelling though my art it's a joy,

I don't even call it painting it's not just a hobby it's a way of expressing my mood and a way to see my life and the way I see life around me. I really enjoy people watching as the shapes and movement really inspire me. Showing my observations of how you live your life striping back the technologies of modern life back to the very beginning is hinted at in every image captured.

THE MOTHER'S DIVERSE ROLES

"It's fitting that this vision of "Mother" has the colours of many nation's flags. Mother of the nation has power in this view."

You can visit my website www.djiboart.co.uk to see the original colour.

Go on everyone has a view of what is shown. Is it your Mum? Stop laughing! No seriously look beyond the clothes, really look at the image.

So again, anything that hints at your Mum?

The mood colours posture maybe?

Anyway, let's get on and ask a few questions of you the Visitors to this frozen moment in time.

Who looked after you as the world developed around you?

Who gave you that look but still asked if you were hungry?

Who was the centre of calm whilst all around was chaos?

Yep it's a vision of a woman loaded with as much as one can carry.

But there is much more if you allow your mind to connect with the messages imprinted in your eyes.

"God won't give you too much to carry only what your shoulders can bear."

Wise words from my mum as I worried about this and that that growing up brings. You must look into the vision. Climb into the scene. Now look around where are the plants the trees the buildings the things that make up a community?

The trappings of society that support life?

No nothing in sight.

What is mother carrying?

Many levels to explore let's take a few. Leaving a relationship, leaving a society that doesn't want them, leaving a life of lost hope? Or shall we say on their way to new beginnings?

A new start a new world a long journey where there is no land until you arrive.

In some way shape or form, we have all been immigrants. We have left for better lives and new dreams.

The centre of our dreams is that our mothers, the women who care and watch over us teach us through soft skills that the world if treated with respect will reward us with the life we sow.

This is my homage to all mothers and womankind.

Take away all the technology we cannot live without and this mother showed is the mother that history will recall.

For even when all physical comforts are taken, a mother has bags of support for her children to feed on. So yes, bags and such are show, so now you have another way of looking.

Should we instead of looking, see with emotion and interpret past memories through the vision shown?

So once again the question, which part of the whole fits your mum in the vision shown?

Go on give your mum a hug and let her know you love her as that is the fuel that makes her sacrifices pale into a smile.

LADIES GOING SHOPPING

When we are going shopping no one really likes to go on their own, though maybe sometimes hahahaha. I noticed one particular day and if I am honest, from a very early age, it kind of struck me that my mum always went shopping with either a friend a bunch of like-minded or with us children, very rarely on her own. Some really see it as a weakness. When going shopping whether male or female, you like going with your friends so I created a particular painting that sums up fond memories that reminded me of my mum when it was time to go shopping. I had to tag along as her porter and for her friends too.

An idea came to mind whilst creating, what happens on the other side of the world? Is this something we always did when shopping throughout history?

I asked myself about the Caribbean and Africa do they use shopping bags and I thought of the vessels that carry water on their heads and such like. Why don't we? Is it any less dignified to carry your shopping bags instead of dragging them along the floor? Shouldn't we put them on our heads because it straightens our back? It could be why we have so many back problems, because of carrying things in the wrong manner.

When you look at my paintings yes, they are carrying vessels upon their heads and it may look as a backwards kind of life but it's a healthy kind of life, isn't it?

It is a healthy kind of life, yeah, so that's where my inspiration Ladies shopping comes from.

WHAT CELEBRATING DIVERSITY MEANS

Whenever I leave my home, I see diversity all around me whether in Stamford Cambridge London it doesn't matter. I see it in everything around me and people don't actually take it on board I try to encapsulate it in everything that I produce.

I will give you an example a couple of weeks ago I was in the centre of Peterborough where we were gathering people to a summer Fete at the Visitors Centre, where information about the happenings around the city can be obtained.

The general public turned stopped and joined in the hustle and bustle of Caribbean music and were treated to paintings of all kinds of vibrant colours. They wore all kinds of exciting outfits different languages all together for one moment in time all the different cultures in the Peterborough were in one place. Every day these cultures walk past each other, and they don't really connect, but for one moment all you needed to know about diversity was on show.

My workshops for example, I put such elements together music food and art, and the common denominator that brings all races and creeds together is this mix that makes us all smile and the barriers to diversity fall away.

It was like a Nexus, all you need is one common denominator to call people together. We had gathered complete strangers in the middle of the street. I mean Tuesday morning who in their right mind dances in the middle of the pavement or street. Few walked by with a frown on their face, for that brief moment in time my paintings captured a moment of their time, people smiling talking to each other whether Spanish Portuguese English Italian or polish they were chatting even if you are different, one common denominator it was fun it was music.

I was like a child being inquisitive "what was going on there?" We all have a nosey nature. I really believe that if we could find a way to bring people together it will be in that kind of a format. We will not solve the problems of the world, but we can put the smile which is better than the frown. Thank you!

People said to me Roland; why are you always smiling?

Where do you get so much energy?

well not being funny its less work grumpy is so taxing told you I have a different way of looking at my world.

Can I give an example of how I think as an artist about it?

Inclusion to me is when I am trying to show people where I come from and trying to take them where they come from and then creating a melting pot of art in an image and from that I have developed some workshops where it doesn't matter if you are old young blind whatever, a common sense or vision colour story ties all sides together. I try to include everything that I have, just to give you a hint, a little bit is done to tease them I want them to let go of their own inhibitions to be the part of my inclusion moment in time everything I do is part of the parcel of time my idea is always to bring my life experiences and theirs and like jam spread it as on the bread of life, from this we are creating something, and that's what inclusion is for me it brings everything together in my case it's something in the strokc of a paint brush pen or charcoal and creating something out of it and together when they a piece of me goes with them, does that make sense?

DIVERSITY AND THE NEGATIVE SPACE

I can actually give you lots of answers as compared to the people you asked this question before me, it's quite simple I have to talk it through my art because I live and breathe sleep and dream in every one of my images I can actually show a sample of what diversity is I've used an Eastern European vision depicting Diversity in bloodshed across many cultures.

However, I've learnt from them about where they come from I am trying to put it on canvas I can actually adapt to diversity in the world at the moment it is all about emphasizing people's differences inferring it is wrong why?

I thought diversity was there to make things stronger for all. In my artwork, I am saying yeah, I am British! What I have is my background, what is yours?

Where we have common ground and I put it all in one place so when you look at something... oh you can see African there you can see a bit of aaha that's from that city you can spot that I am using different elements that people find in one place that's diversity for me it's not about being frightened looking for conflict.

Why do you think people got into the frightened state?

There's a new one that I have heard the use of the word frightened so we have to explore it a little bit so what is causing that in the world Community that causes the fear in the people? If I said information overload would that make sense?

This is a world where news is virtual instant live streaming, so imagine the scenario of a play ground you have one little gang around, you always know top dog there, and another little gang that acts normally in daily life and that little gang says *"I don't like your hat"* a person from the other Gang answers *"why do you not like my hat?"*

This starts a retaliation; *"I don't like your trousers. I don't like your shoes"* which soon gets worse and personal. *Religion teaches us that the world is the same yet, we are not all the same. We migrated around the world,* we developed safety systems to protect ourselves, so we fear the unknown.

If we knew more about each other, we would have less to fear. We have lost the ability to sit in front of someone and talk to them we are very much into talking online etc. We are losing the ability to read people's facial expressions and making wrong assumptions on where their mind is, so the written word is sometimes interpreted in the wrong way more than verbal.

For me, that is where the fear comes from. If you don't know something, rather than trying to find out what it's all about; you will follow the rest of the sheep. So that gang over there hates this gang over there. The term 'gang'; we associate the term gang with violence. In the old days' gangs were tribes and tribes looked out for each other. It was the family unit where you were meant to feel safe was at the forefront of all the values stood.

What's that word? Fragmented? You should actually talk to someone about it instead of *whatever.*

MOTHER'S LIGHT PAINTING AND DIVERSITY

'Mothers light'

Traditions transitions cultures and Diversity in a vision and real life created from a deeply personal moment in my life.

Only two dark paintings have I ever produced, and this is a very poignant one.

You the viewer, what comes to mind on first sight?

What colours caught you first?

What if any memories did it trigger?

What emotion/s did it stir if any?

With all the vibrancy in my previous work, why on earth would such a creation pour from my brush and seduce your vision for but a small moment of your time?

Why and where was my mind for this to come forth?

Understanding me just a little might help answer. Emotion is a key element in creating parcels of time and visions of my world. It's why I only work in small parcels of time as it can be very exhausting trying to maintain the muse.

This was evident in this particular vision, as my emotions were very raw brutal and dark in their intensity.

In the midst was a light that guided me home to sanity and peace of mind.

One that I know with dread will one day leave for a better place.

My father was dying. I knew it but the rest of my family didn't want to see or hear that.

Everyday a piece of light left him in words memories and mobility.

The man who protected me from the realities of real life was leaving and his light which showed me the way would be replaced by the torch that was my mum.

How do I honour his legacy and that of my mum? How do I show all the fear the hate the sacrifices they made to protect and give us the gifts to face the world that had turned its back on them?

"Look and learn"

The darkness is where we originated. It in this world is the fear of those that are different yet the same, the hatred of the unknown the indifference to basic humility the struggles to work to put food on tables clothes on backs and worst of all slaves to the system that keeps us there.

At some point I am not sure when, the light in my eyes as a child took be back to the dark days of my childhood, and there my mother was the light of love reassurance comfort stability, just a few things all mothers have, and that helped me find my way and recognise that it's the power of mothers that in all ills lead us to smile again.

In my despair, the brush led me to create the three mantras that form my daily life.

Mischief, mayhem and chaos. Yes, all are there in the dark void yet the colours in the figures also have those qualities, but they carry the gift of hope.

Use these three to bring joy a smile and the world is your friend.

So, my viewer, the chaos is the colour of a mothers' garment against the darkness. Be it a smile a cuddle a word of encouragement a simple look. The mayhem is the way our chattels are carried/ No laptop bags or taxi.

And mischief are the children teasing each other on the opening journey ahead.

If you are not smiling at this, then you're still in the dark.

So from pain joy is the reward if we look hard enough.

Yes, a dark painting. A parcel a moment of time in the grand quilt that is life.

For me, it is the journey of my family throughout their histories. The dark lands to the light of possibilities.

So viewer where are your experiences in here?

Do you have memories that invoke deep emotions?

Did you spot the tears we all shed at some point in our lives?

Who popped into your mind as you read the story?

You too are in my story and I thank you for being part of the walk in the paths these colours embody.

What I am trying to show in my paintings is to see through the eyes of that person. If I point you towards one of my paintings. The painting above which I call **'mothers light'.** I painted it because I was frightened that my dad was dying. **The Mother's light is blue. You can visit my website www.djiboart.co.uk to see the original colour.**

If you look around the edges, that was all the fears that we ever have in our lives.

It is the fear of losing someone very close.

It could be the fear that you will not be accepted in your particular society.

It is the fear of hatred that's been thrown around you.

I have painted two dark pictures in my life, the mother's light is the second one. What it represents is as you can see when you look at the image is. You have the Mother and two siblings. Also look again; can you see the third child? The one on the mother's back. All of them are looking in one direction. If you're looking at the colouring the lighter blue around the mother that is the ray of light. It is the sunshine that is the beginning of light. For me that's true, that is knowledge and personally, I have always gotten over my falls my fears by going back to very basic why they are frightened of me.

Why I always have three reasons and answers. It could be; they don't understand me it, could be that my looks, or it could be my colour. The classic example is growing up in school where I was used to being bullied. I went home one day from school at the age of seven. I ran upstairs, and I locked myself in the bathroom and my mum thought I was probably dirty. You know mothers they care a lot.

Anyway, I was upstairs for quite some time and my mum went upstairs knocked on the door. She found me in the bath with a scrubbing brush; I was trying to rub the colour off myself. I learnt a very important lesson that day. It was such a traumatic event, but my mum told me *"this is a lesson for you. They fear you. They don't understand you, and it's not your colour that they are frightened of."*

Try to explain this to a seven-year-old didn't work well obviously, however, later in life when I started developing my artwork which embodied such lessons. I finally understood what she was saying that fear is what clouds our reasoning.

After that day, I was able go back to school and whenever anyone called me names, my mum taught me to use the English language in a way that it was either a foil or a shield to protect me. Going forward, if somebody called me stupid, I learnt what the word meant, so I would say *"so you mean I am cleverer than you hahaha?"*

Do you know what that word means?

It could be used as insult or a way to show your intelligence. In Greek and Latin, it means very clever. I learnt how to use my colour to my advantage if I needed to. I learned to use their fear as a way to teach them that if they knew me, they would not fear me. The people that were bullying me became my friends.

Turning Negative Situations into Positive.

The lesson I give to anybody on how to turn those negative situations into positive situation? I use my art as a way of helping me get through life ups and downs. I have never ever had the hassle of walking around with the world's problem of not liking me because at the end of the day, if they don't understand me, it's my responsibility actually to turn their heads to help them find the answers.

My art is not just paintings, it is about telling real-life stories, that is why when anyone asks about my world the first thing I say is *"I am a storyteller but stories in colours"* My mum used to say; *"you don't paint Roland you tell stories in colours"* one of my many phrases is: Passion in a brush.

The Passion in the Brush

I have a particular painting style that incorporates some influences leaned over my life. I am very much into Neolithic Caribbean and African art, and through my many travels Eastern European is one I find very alluring and so on. I put them all together to be used one day as I always had an idea, to teach children that were shy are withdrawn have problems fitting in, on how to find a way to become the person that is hidden inside.

Even those suffering difficulties speaking even dementia for example. I went back to my early childhood where my mum used to teach me my alphabets because my mum was very clever lady obviously when they came to UK they didn't have a lot of money so we used whatever came to hand and that is that mum used, and utilised those techniques to deliver in workshops where the only rule was free your mind and brush or draw with passion.

I learned my times table from a comb. I learnt how to retain my alphabet with a piece of string and a clothes peg. Yes, that is what I said a comb a piece of string and a clothes peg. Ok, I hear you laughing and giggling.

Children like to investigate they want to know, but as an adult, we know you have to do things this way and not that way! We are trapped in the adult world and are shy of giving in to our inner child. It is like putting our imagination in a box and if you are too imaginative then you are a problem being annoying or inquisitive It is too much for a teacher or parent to contend with.

The way I do my workshops is there is only one rule the only rule is your imagination should go out of the window and you transport it onto the piece of paper. So tell me yeah, I can see the number seven, I can see that D or P or whatever and that is what I try to show in my art in my images. I am trying to encourage you to the be free and think like a child to have a moment in time you yourself immerse into one of my paintings which is now your painting what is the first thing that happens in your mind when see a painting. Here is what one buyer, Amina said about the painting she bought from me:

> *"it took me back home it took me back to my family*
> *it makes me very emotional to seeing it yeah it makes*
> *me feel like you been where I grew up"*

All are from stories that my parents my aunts my grandparents told me of their lives their history I have done taken them and mixed with my history my life the people around me the traditions that I have incorporated should we say imprinted in my life it refreshes and invigorates me. That's why I want to show the people yes, I am different I walk around and put my finger on my head to release all the spirits of those long gone behind me and I become the common denominator the conduit that even for a moment brings the diversity of a crowd together.

> "find the common denominator in everything
> you see that's another good quotes wow."

CHILDHOOD AND CELEBRATING DIVERSITY

I have a friend called John and I have had another friend called Gerald when we were kids when we used to hang out with each other, oh dear me it's quite a funny story, John his parents were Scottish, and they were real Scots they hated everything that was English.

John always come to look around my house because he loved our cooking and I used to go their home because I loved his mums cooking and his mum for me was the best cook I have ever seen, besides my mum of course. John's mum made a crust that melted upon your tongue, the beef thick with a rich aromatic onion gravy that trickled along the edge of the large serving spoon used to deliver heaven onto my plate. A steak and kidney pie and the beef came from Scotland, brought down by his dad after watching Celtic at home matches. He chose to buy the beef from Scotland believe it or not that's another story the point is that she reminded me of my mum the white version of my mum, if I am allowed to say that.

Upon entering their home for the first time, their kitchen had an old-fashioned kitchen range the fire was in use, the smell of food the pie and mashed potato and from the very first time I tasted, it was in heaven. Whenever I could, I used the excuse to do my homework at Johns as I always got fed ha-ha and one day my mum said: *"why you always at Jones house?"*

I couldn't tell her that they give me pie so I said we do homework and as we get older it turned out that his mum always complained to John as to why he was always around in my house because he used to like my mum's cooking, sweet potatoes and that kind of thing and Gerald was jealous of us because he lived far away and I teased him with slices of the pie if ever we met up, and when John left our house with a chicken leg or something like that or a bit of black pudding every time we played football John would tease him too.

Three Musketeers was our nickname. I have memories of whenever I was down his mum used to talk and soothe my fears, things I could not talk to my mum about; I was bullied at school because I was the only black person, so she feeds me pieces of pie quite strange. I don't remember the rest of the food on the plate, but I remember she cared for me as if I was one of her own. After she passed away, I learnt she deliberately make the pie for me so whenever I have my steak and kidney pie, I think of John's mum.

KIDNEY PIE AND PLANTAIN ON THE CHICKEN

"Kidney pie of John's house and plantain on the chicken at my house: the beauty of celebrating our diversity?"

Simple, isn't it? Friendships from different continents they cross all the political divide something as simple as plate of food a pie and in a sense, I am trying to replicate that in my artwork.

"These are just two young boys who are just enjoying being different from different angles of the spectrum and just loving it. Just going for it and that is so refreshing because you could easily say that we don't eat pie at my house, and he could have easily said the same about your chicken. Your mums also could have stopped you or said we don't eat that kind of food.

"In all honesty, those are the things that make me appreciate celebrating diversity. The reason why I want the people to tell their stories. For you, you could just see that situation as a simple situation, but when you actually think it through, it is a very essence of this book. The essence of celebrating the diversity on your families, even as young as you were"
- Amina Chitembo

It's very basic or it could be very complicated and if you teach someone from a simple item pen, pieces of string what they create you can learn about their culture and your culture. I am so passionate about my workshops in schools and no matter what governments think and whatever they say the funding is being is squeezed so I decided to do something about it I realized that some schools didn't actually have dedicated art in their schools I found myself actually donating some of my paints and brushes.

I asked myself why I am doing it we have companies out there that say they are socially responsible I thought to myself ok I am going to see how responsible you are so with the aid of Peterborough Community Radio. I decided to do an art competition I described a piece of my artwork over the air waves, and the idea was the children listening to it would have to replicate what they thought they heard but at the same time, put a number and a letter in their creation and on the other half of the promotion.

I will get the local businesses to donate and sponsor the aired competition in that way Schools could have access to funds to develop their art classes one of the companies donated the use of a building for couple of weeks, so I could exhibit the students artwork we got sponsors in, and the whole idea was to get the parents on board that if they don't shout out for their schools they would lose their art and music not every school can afford an art teacher not every school can afford a music teacher.

Art should be about how you could encourage a child to be free and express themselves and still be part of a team that they feel nothing is holding them back that was the idea and it got was so well supported. The winners were displayed in the Visitors centre for two weeks. Some of the children were enlightened and their parents. I have a letter from a parent who said:

"I didn't know that my child was creating such artwork" and we have an instance where one of the parents wrote to their school and the school wrote back to me stating the parent now wanted to take their child into the different exhibitions and take them out to experience the different forms of Arts. So, from that little idea of trying to enlightened people by art is the centre of all we do for me that made me rich inside I get richness from the seeds I planted and that will grow, and they then take a little bit of me.

In the workshops, I gave them examples of the history about particular regions that we are working on, about language, a bit of about where people came from. I asked the children a little bit about their history. Then I asked them to incorporate in their drawings their favourite number or letter. That's why I have this innate feeling and desire that I will not only become an artist to create images, but I want to become a teacher through my heart the art is the centre no matter where you are in the world if you don't have the imagination if you are not allowed to express yourself ,fear takes place doesn't it, and an engineer to express his ideas he draws them, to demonstrate them in some shape or form imagine if we didn't have access to even basic art.

WORK IN THE SCHOOLS

You would be surprised at how tight the budgets are that's why if I don't sell my pieces of Arts I can't subsidise my prices to schools to deliver workshops we all have to make a living and I figured it out that I am offering a very low price I am making sure that my prices are at the level that schools can afford. so ensuring all students have access to my services as none should be excluded.

They should have the right to express themselves and it shouldn't be dictated by penny-pinching bean counters. We seem to be in a society where everything is controlled by a standard monetary value

I have even created sensory table no one has to be turned away from it "I am sorry that because you are in a chair, or poor of sight" or whatever not able to access my art workshops that's why I created the sensory table so I can provide classes for all children they stand or sit in their wheel chairs around the same table and create different pieces of artwork.

All the students have to close their eyes ha-ha they learn how to draw with their eyes closed and draw on wallpaper. The idea is very simple different textures on the table and the student have to run their hands on it with their eyes closed and create an image it could be a landscape or animal may be a figure is in their mind they have no more than 5 minutes to touch the table then they quickly go inside the class and then replicate that image on the paper. and that's what I do in my sensory classes I am trying to encourage the student to let them their imagination go wild forget the boundaries and draw whatever comes to mind. They actually enjoy the ensuing results. Children have really strong imaginations.

FINAL WORDS

"I want people to understand that first glance
should not be your only glance on everything in life."

I have three tasks; If I use the analogy about fear you are not sure about someone and you just look at them you can turn this feeling into a positive one my mum used to say

"Roland they are three things you must do every single day, treat them to a little bit of Mischief, Chaos."

Can you guess what is the third one is?

"Mayhem" hahaha. Yes, mayhem but do it in a way that doesn't harm anybody, and your objective is to make them smile.

Smile: so make someone smile every day, every day make someone smile whether you have been mischievous make them smile if you have created chaos make them smile but you do in a fun way and if you see someone having a bad day you should make them smile maybe mayhem could be I don't know pretend to trip or something like that or talking to them in a funny voice. People like it when I use the voice of my mum. Make a fool of yourself and the moment you see them smiling your task is complete. Never look back with a frown I lived by those three rules every day and for me, I like smiling.

When I had an event in the city centre once, I danced with the public who were killing themselves laughing that was my mischief of the day.

Chaos: another aim was to get into the middle of a crowd just joking about to disperse them, and they all started laughing and joking that was my chaos.

Mayhem: mayhem was the fun I had with the pebble painting.

My hope is that this insight into my journey gives you a different way of looking at life. Whoever you are reading this book, I bet your story is as diverse as mine.

So when will we read yours?

Lucy Oyubo

 ucy is a CEO and a Founder of Hakuna Matata Language and Cultural Exchange in Basel, Switzerland, where she also lives. She a qualified Interpreter and a translator. She interprets and translates Swahili, English and German in different Institutions and in court, in Basel, Zurich and Bern.

She holds a Bachelor of Education (B. ED) from Kenyatta University in Nairobi, Kenya with a major in Swahili and Philosophy of Religious Studies. Her first school in Switzerland was called; 'Lakeside English Centre' she taught English and Swahili.

In 2010 she founded Hakuna Matata Language and Cultural Exchange with the help of the Gründungszentrum Crescenda, an organization that promotes female immigrant entrepreneurship in Basel. In 2015 she was awarded the Company of the Year Award by the African Woman in Europe (AWE) organisation.

Area of Expertise: Teaching, Interpreting and Translating

Books: (1) Das Crescenda-Modell, (2.) The perfect Migrant.

Contact Details:

LinkedIn - https://www.linkedin.com/in/lucy-oyubo

Facebook - http://bit.do/LOyubo

Phone - +41(0)76 578 4555

Email - lylum22@yahoo.com

Websites - www.suaheli-lernen.ch

A Swahili Teacher in Switzerland

By Lucy Oyubo

"My slogan is Hakuna Matata, take it easy, no matter what!"

MY PROFESSIONAL LIFE AND LOVE FOR LANGUAGES

Having acquired a Bachelor of Education, majoring in Swahili and Philosophy of Religious Studies at Kenyatta University in Kenya, I was employed to teach Swahili and Religious Education at Olkejuado High School in Kajiado. Kajiado, is a small town in Masai Land, situated about 85 Km from the Kenya's capital, Nairobi. I enjoyed teaching such young and intelligent boys very much. I was happy and grateful for the contribution I was making to the younger generation of my country because that was priceless for me.

If I had managed to do my master's in public health in Australia, maybe I would be in a different profession right now but I believe my call to be a teacher was real.

My wish to continue to teach Swahili and English after moving to Switzerland was fulfilled. I got a job six month after moving here to teach at Volkshochschule in Romanshorn. The lady who was running the school gave her notice and I was left with so many students to look after. That is how my private teaching started and the idea of opening a school came about. I first taught them privately in my living room for a while before opening.

I then took this opportunity to develop myself further. I did the Certificate of English Language Teaching to Adults course (CELTA) at Stanton Teachers College in 2006 in London, which was a necessary step. To be able to be recognised as a Language Teacher in Switzerland, I also did Schweizerischer Verband für Erwaschsene Bildung (SVEB) in Zürich. It is a pre-requisite if one intends to teach in this country.

When I got back from London, I got a beautiful room by the Lake Constance with the help of Alice Huber, one of my students. And I rented it. I was quite proud to be able to open the school in this country, and named it, "The Lakeside English Centre", a perfect name for the school, as located by the Lake.

My reasons to continue to teach Swahili and English were to enhance my cultural knowledge and understanding of others but also to share my own culture with others, in a way. This was fuelled by my desire to continue to follow my passion and to contribute to the lives of the Swiss people here, as I did back in Kenya. While teaching privately, I also gave lessons at other institutions, like teaching English in Benedict-Schule in St. Gallen and Business English at a company in Romanshorn called EFTEC, and also Sekundarschule in Romanshorn. I consider myself very lucky to have been able to follow my passion as well as help others in their quest for knowledge and understanding.

Over a period of seven years, thousands of students have passed through my school, learning mainly English. I also had some private students, who drove from Zürich, an hour away, to come and learn Swahili, my language. I was very proud of them, as well as of myself for making it possible.

What touches my heart the most is the fact that it's been more than 10 years since I closed the school, but when I visit the area and meet my former students, I have learned that they are still keep in touch with each other. For instance, there are 2 groups which still meet once a week up to this day.. I cannot be proud enough, and they keep thanking me for bringing them together.

After my divorce, I moved to Basel in 2009. I did not get any financial help from my ex-husband Martin, so I stayed put for 3 months, looking for ways to earn my living here. I was forced to seek Social Benefit during that time, until I found a job with Sprachschule Baselland (SBL) where I taught English, and with Pro-Senectute in Baselstadt where I taught Swahili. I was lucky to also get some University students whom I taught Swahili privately. It touched my heart that they wanted to learn the language just for fun.

Things started working well for me. I was able to join Lingua-dukt (HEKS) and do a course to be able to carry out interpretation and translation work in hospitals, schools and social facilities. This was a big blessing for me. At the same time, I was made aware about Crescenda, an organization that promotes female-immigrant entrepreneurship in Basel. I attended a course in 2014 with them, where we were taught marketing, legal issues and finances, in parallel with Intercultural Interpretation course.

I had run the Lakeside English Centre without any prior knowledge on these important aspects. These provided me with the inspiration I needed, and led me to open in Basel the "Hakuna Matata Language Centre "which I have lately changed to "Hakuna Matata Language and Cultural Exchange. Thanks to the support of Crescenda, which also offered a room to rent in their building, the school was born.

It is important to note that German is the language of instruction at Crescenda; so one is required to speak it quite well. If you live in or around Basel, Switzerland and are thinking of starting your own busincss, feel free to google www.crescenda.ch and get further information.

Hakuna Matata Language and Cultural Exchange

Hakuna Matata Language and Cultural Exchange was then born after the course. I teach Swahili, English, German, guide African Tours in Basel. I give Swahili dishes cooking lessons to those who may be interested in "learning by doing" as my students learn my rich African culture. Living in the German-speaking part of Switzerland motivated me to work hard and perfect my German so that I could be able to teach the language as well. It is a pretty difficult language, so I am actually still working hard on it. It is also difficult to Swiss speakers themselves. Since they have to learn it here like a subject, the way we learn English in schools in Kenya. It is also the official language in the German speaking part of Switzerland, just like English is in Kenya.

I also found a Swahili teaching Job at the University of Basel and was quite happy to teach my language and my culture to loving stud**ents. I enjoyed it for** 2 years. Later, there was no much demand for it and Swahili stopped being offered at the Language Centre.

Since I have done interpretation in German, Swahili and English. Because I have already done interpretation work, I wanted to go a step further. I then got a job and could interpret in the public prosecutor's office in Basel Land, but without having done a course to be officially recognised. My aim was to be able to interpret and translate in court. In order to do this, I had to pass a very difficult exam. I can say I am so proud of myself because I did pass the exam.

I now interpret in courts in Switzerland as a part-time, and at the same time I run my school. My school was awarded the Company of the Year Award by African Woman in Europe (AWE 2015).

MY LOVELY EXPERIENCE AS A SWAHILI AND ENGLISH TEACHER.

I was very proud of myself that I was able to open a school, a year after coming to Switzerland named, "The Lakeside English Centre". My reason to teach Swahili and English after moving here was to enhance my culture in a way and this was fuelled by my desire to continue following my passion and contributing to the lives of my students like I did back in Kenya.

A lot of people ask me, "Who the hell in Basel wants to learn Swahili"

Actually, there are doctors, nurses, going to work in hospitals in East Africa, people married to the natives of East Africa, as well ethnology, archaeology or literature students. I have taught those who have had lessons with me simply because they feel Swahili is a beautiful language that can be learnt easily and do it just for fun.

The feedback I got from my students was that they were always looking forward to coming to my classes because I did not only teach grammar but gave explanations about cultural differences and also my own experience in their country.

Most students told me how they were always looking forward to seeing how I dressed up when they came to class. My mixture of cultural and modern dressing fascinated them.

I still get this compliment from my current students. The best part of my students were elderly, so they were happy to learn in an easier and in a fun way. My method of teaching is learning by doing. We go to restaurants to practice the language whereby they order in whatever language they are learning.

We go to the Zoo to see and learn names of animals. We travelled to London to practice English several times when I was running the Lakeside English Centre.

We cook Swahili dishes learning the names of the ingredients and different types of foods, depending on the language the students are learning. This also happens when I invite my students to my home, or we are invited by one of the students to their homes, and I keep insisting we speak in English or Swahili depending on the language they are learning.

What makes my teaching even more rewarding to me and my students here in Switzerland is, for instance, when some of my students come back from a trip to East Africa., They come to see me in order to narrate their experience and their positive encounters with the natives. Their stories and how happy they have been to able to communicate and make the natives happy always touch my heart. An example was when one of my students, Heidi, was stopped by police with an unstrapped seat belt at the back of the car in Tanzania; she made the police officer laugh like crazy when she suddenly thought of my slogan and said, 'Tafadhali polisi, Hakuna Matata'. I always tell them to use the slogan Hakuna Matata on whatever situation they find themselves in and it has always worked. Like when they get pestered by the natives to give them money I tell them to say, ' Sina pesa, mimi ni Mzungu maskini'. The natives of the country they are visiting do not believe their ears and they all end up having a laugh.

The other reason why I was motivated to open my own school was the little pay I received when I first taught in a few schools in and around Basel. I am quite happy to be the only one running a Swahili school in Switzerland. I loved the language even in school and learnt it to the level of the University. I learnt its history, culture and its beauty. I am quite honoured to continue teaching it here. I did give more English lessons in my first school. Basel has a lot of schools teaching English, so I am concentrating on teaching Swahili.

I believe it is my purpose to empower and teach more people how to speak and read Swahili in a powerful way, and in a way that they will fall in love with the language and never forget it, plus their experiences using the language`. At the moment I am concentrating on both Interpreting, translating and teaching at my school.

MY EXPERIENCE LEARNING A NEW LANGUAGE

I remember going to the supermarkets with my teeny weeny dictionary when I was still quite new in Switzerland. German is a very difficult language. One has to know whether a noun is feminine, masculine or neutral. The verbs are divided into datives and accusatives. One has to learn which verbs are reflexive, which I still find quite amusing.

And then, for example, the English word "the", which luckily enough does not even exist in Swahili, has 3 words in German, "der", "die", and "das". and this is according to the gender, whether feminine, masculine or neutral. One has to learn all this off head.

My big problem was the pronunciation of the letters è, ü ö, ä and w. I am sure this is a problem to most learners. You may not be understood if you pronounce the word wrongly. I tend to use these letters unnecessarily. I remember hiking in the Swiss alps one time with some friends.

There was no network at some point and I told a friend, "Pass auf, Ich habe kein Empfängnis hier" /Listen, I do not have conception here. I should have said, pass auf, "Ich habe kein Empfang hier /I should not have network here. My friend laughed and told me if I wanted to conceive and get a baby? These two words have very different meanings. Empfang is reception, and Empfängnis is conception.

When I went to the supermarkets to buy some food I would pronounce some words wrongly and no one would understand me. I loved it when workers looked at me like an alien and would sometimes alert several other workers and ask each other if they spoke English and could understand what I was asking for. Because of this, I carried my dictionary to show them the word and they would go like ahuh.

The best part was when I wanted to get rid of coins and went to the till to pay. Then the cashier goes like, "sexfrankenfünfunfünzik", and then I would go like, what? They could repeat a hundred times for all I cared, but all I did was pour all the coins on the till for them to pick the amount they needed. This went on for a long time and I was having lots of fun with the Swiss language.

I read children's books as a beginner which I borrowed from the library. You should do the same if you are a newcomer. They are easy to understand.

I was very proud to say, "Danke vielmals"/ thank you and "Auf Wiedersehen" /goodbye, which is what one has to first learn after landing in this country. The Swiss always say Grüezi/hi and goodbye wherever they go. And they are amongst the few Europeans who greet and kiss each other 3 times. Many countries like Germany and French do it twice.

I listened to the radio and watched television. I watched lots of German talk shows like those held by Barbara Salesch and Stefan Raab, whose talk shows could sometimes be full of laughs, fights and bad words.

I didn't have the chance to practice my German at home because Martin didn't like speaking it, his reason being, we met speaking English and we should continue doing the same. I regretted later. I could have asked for a win-win situation. Whereby I could speak to him in German and he replied in English. We could both have been happy.

I kept smiling at the occasions when I spontaneously spoke to him in public in German and he answered in English and he was looked at by people wondering what his problem was. I urge those who are having the same problem with their partners not to give up but compromise on a win-win situation. If you live in the German-speaking area of Switzerland, you will only feel better if you can speak German.

When I taught English to beginners at Volkshochschule, Romanshorn, some students didn't sometimes understand what I was saying. They wanted me to explain in German, but I couldn't. At that time, I could speak very little German. Unfortunately, some of them became quite frustrated and left. I fully understood their frustration because I had had a similar experience back in Kenya.

I joined a beginner's French class at Alliance Francaise in Nairobi way back in 1995. I couldn't speak a word of French, but my teacher spoke French in class, throughout. I decided to quit. This method makes life easy if one is not a total beginner.

Thus, I did understand the students who quit and their action encouraged me to work double harder to learn this truly difficult language. I am still learning it and I know this will be for the rest of my life. People keep on telling me how I speak good German, but my answer is usually even the Germans themselves make mistakes, and the Swiss are even worse in the Language. They are only comfortable with their Swiss dialects.

I resisted learning Swiss German because we have many cantons in the German-speaking part of Switzerland and each canton has its own dialect. I lived in the Thurgau canton which has a different dialect from the one spoken in Basel. I could understand a lot of what was said but couldn't speak it. Then I moved to Basel and I understood zero. If I had moved to Geneva for example, I would not have needed to understand the dialect at all. I personally feel it is a waste of time to learn Swiss German because if I go to Wallis, which is a Canton in Switzerland, that has a special dialect, no one will understand me. Considering the fact that even Swiss natives have a problem understanding it.

Since everyone in this country speaks high German why bother? The most important reason why I would never want to learn Swiss German at this juncture is because I met so many immigrants who made the mistake of learning Swiss German in the beginning after arriving here. It is now so hard for them to speak high German, which is the official language in the German-speaking area. Some of them cannot differentiate some words in Swiss German and high German and unfortunately cannot even write German. My advice goes especially to those newcomers living in Switzerland. I advise them to concentrate on learning high German first, before learning Swiss German because everyone speaks German and you can be understood by people around you.

I read children books as a beginner which I borrowed from the library. You should do the same if you are a newcomer.

They are easy to understand.

Also, what helped me a lot to master the language was when I talked and made mistakes I didn't get discouraged. I continued talking and talking; I practiced as much as I could. I always begged people to correct me. There are times when not all my questions could be answered because the people around me didn't know the answer themselves, but I never gave up. This is the advice I give my students which is also important to all of us.

How many Americans or British people speak other languages?

One should be proud to speak more than one language. That is the reason one should not shy away from making mistakes. The Swiss people are experts in this. Many Swiss people do speak very good English or French but if you ask them they say no. If you continue talking to them, you realise they lack confidence and are afraid of making mistakes. So, I do make sure I drill this point to my students such that they overcome their fear. I love it when they just blabber away and make mistakes and have themselves corrected, because then they remember the correction and learn from it. The correct stuff.

I understand how difficult the language is but with lots of effort and following the tips I have given above you can make it.

How Amazing Cultural Differences Can Be.

In Swahili, we only have one word 'Panya' for a rat and a mouse. In German Speaking countries, Mausi is a name used just like the English couple say 'honey,' or 'sweetheart'. So, when I first arrived in Switzerland, Martin was so happy to call me Mausi. I asked him what it meant, and when he said it means a mouse, I immediately thought of those ugly rats and mice at home and vehemently resisted being called a Mausi. I asked him to remember the sight of the rats and mice he had seen back in Kenya and he understood my reaction.

My fellow Africans, imagine how your friends and family back home would react when you visited them with your spouse from Europe, then they keep calling you 'Mausi' and they request to know what it means. I preferred him calling me "Spätzli", which means kidege in Swahili which is a little bird. "Kidege" is used in the famous Swahili song, "Malaika, nakupenda Malaika". I have lived in Europe for ages but will never ever imagine keeping a rat, a mouse or even a snake as pets like some people do here. I would be accused of being a witch if I were in Kenya.

Here, in Switzerland, people eat soup and do not drink it like we say in Kenya. So, imagine visiting a friend in Nairobi and saying, I am not hungry today, can we just eat some soup?

«Sihisi njaa leo, tunaweza kula supu tu?» This would be so strange too in Switzerland if someone said, "Heute bin ich nicht hungrig, trinken wir nur Suppe?"

Soup is mostly served in a bowl or cup back in Kenya while it is mainly served on a plate here. Being married to Martin has made me find this small difference quite thrilling.

Most Swiss people have their dinner at 6:30 pm or earlier. I have not been able to catch up. They do have a good reason for it but personally, I am still fighting. Martin could come home from work and expect to find food on the table by 6:30 pm. To be honest, I am still fighting with this idea. If I had my dinner like even at 8:00 pm I would wake up at midnight hungry, looking for food. This is what most Swiss families do in the evening. Unlike many countries in the South of Europe and also in Kenya where I come from, we eat much later. I have been unable to catch up with that until now.

When my parents visited me in 2006. We then went out for dinner, whereby my mom Mathilda watched other guests eating fresh mixed salad. She is full of humour because she asked, "Why are people chewing raw grass like cows in this country". I couldn't help laughing because since we didn't eat raw salad when I grew up, I found eating raw salad unbelievable when I fast arrived here. We were used to coleslaw. We did not mostly eat raw salad because our water was not good. Little did she know that the salad had sauce in it. So, when I prepared some salad at home and she tasted it, she kept asking for more saying, "It is my turn to be the cow today".

THE WONDER AND FUN IN LANGUAGES

The love of languages made me learn Spanish and French while living in this country. My French is not perfect though. I always make sure I pick up a few important phrases whenever I travel.

Seeing people's reaction of excitement touches my heart. I adore the fact that some words in a language can mean something quite different in another language.

When I was still quite new in Switzerland, Martin made me laugh so hard when he told me this story. Someone in the family was married to a guy from Kenya, from the Kikuyu community. So, one evening they decided to go to the cinema. Then he sees the word "Kino" written in the front of the building. He then stops and said, "

What? I cannot believe my eyes. What the hell would they write such a word here?"

He was lost with words when he was told that it means a cinema in German.

And what is it in Kikuyu?

A lady's private part, he answered.

The other funny thing is that when a man from the Kikuyu ethnic group meets a man from the Kalenjin ethnic group, in Kenya, and asks for his name. The man from the Kalenjin ethnic group answers and says," I am Mr. Keino". The Kikuyu man laughs aloud. Keino is a common Kalenjin surname which also means a lady's private part in Kikuyu.

Furthermore, we have many Italians called Tomba. I remember a famous slalom skier called Alberto Tomba that I met on my first visit to Switzerland when I went with some friends to learn how to ski in Schladming, Austria. I personally couldn't believe my ears, when people cheered him says, "Tomba, Tomba". When I told the people around me it's meaning in Swahili having had a few Gluhweins /hot wine and Jägertee they even screamed harder. Alberto Tomba won the run that night. All the Italians who visit Kenya and are called Tomba have to change their names or only mention the first one unwillingly.

If a Mr Tomba from Italy met his mother-in-law in a village in Kenya and introduced themselves, the lady would run away with shame. He would have to mention his first name. The reason being, the word Tomba means to fuck. Or a Kenyan lady, married to a Mr. Tomba in Italy, introducing herself in front of people in Kenya as Mrs Tomba. This would be hilarious.

A Kenyan student was called to study at Kumamoto University in Japan. Kumamoto is a beautiful city in Japan. Please google www.kumamoto.com. The boy could not have the guts to tell his mom which University he was going to study. His friends knew the name of the university and kept making jokes about how lucky he was. He never got to tell his mom the name of the university. His uncle did it, and the mom realised why. Kuma is a vagina and moto is hot in Swahili. Yes, and if a Japanese from Kumamoto was asked in Kenya or Tanzania which town he comes from, people will of course not believe their ears. This is so interesting.

I guess those reading this page will never forget these words.

This is what fascinates me about languages. It is amazing to see how one word or a phrase in a certain language could mean something quite different, in a different language. Watch out for my book which is about to be published soon.

FINAL WORDS

My final words to you dear reader are:

1. If you want to do something, and you put your mind into it, you will always succeed.
2. Listen to your heart and follow your dream. I wanted to leave my country and go to a land far away right as a child, and I made it.
3. It is never too late in life to learn new things. Those people of colour who cannot swim, cycle, ski, or ice-skate, I would like to assure you that it is never too late in life.

All these things are doable and exciting. I agree that most of these sports are expensive, but I believe everything is possible. Where there is a will, there is a way. Most of us prefer spending our money on drinks and making merry. I urge all those living here to try and engage in different activities. You will be surprised how much fun it is.

4. Those who are still freshers and living in Switzerland. Do not let your boyfriends, husbands, or wives deprive you of your rights and make you live a miserable life. While working as an interpreter, I have realised that there are so many of us immigrants being taken advantage of by our partners. Some partners do not want you to learn German; they do not want you to go out there and meet people because they assumed they would be misled. This is your right, and you are allowed to approach your Gemeinde / municipal council and ask them the way forward. If your partner is earning less money, your German courses could be paid for. Speaking German in this country is very important. Most of us avoid going to social events because we shy off, which is a pity.

   a. I was lucky to marry a man who was very fair to me. Right from the beginning when I was unemployed, there was trust between us. He informed me of everything about his financial status and thus we were able to work together and see the way forward with the little money we had.

   b. He let me do the shopping with his credit card. Most of the ladies or guys from other countries brought here are sometimes treated like shit by their partners. I have witnessed some relationships where partners were quite envious that they couldn't let their spouses even go out dancing or having drinks with friends without a big fight. Many such relationships end up breaking up when the victims realise that they are being denied their rights. Some of my girlfriends didn't know how much their husbands earned, their husbands bought food and dictated what had to be cooked in the house, they chose when to buy them clothes and did everything for them. Not because they liked it but because they didn't trust them at all.

5. They were not even allowed to work, in order to avoid paying more taxes, which is a common thing in Switzerland. For example, it can be much cheaper to stay at home and take care of your child than go to work because getting a nanny is unaffordable

6. I advise you to make sure you stand up for your rights and refuse to feel any kind of intimidation. And ladies, if you have a problem and do not know whom to turn to, find out if there is 'a Frauenhaus' in your area and contact them for help. We have them all over Switzerland.

7. I urge all of you to enjoy the beauty of this country. I urge you to do it. You are very lucky, like I always say, to live in this country. I think it is the land of plenty and not America any more.

8. I am very proud to be doing many good and positives things in this country. Many people believe most African women are prostitutes and fools. We actually have a lot of African Intellectuals in this country who need a lot of support to improve their lives. They would do much better if they were in French or English-speaking countries because the main obstacle they have, just like I did, is the German language.

Acknowledgements

For a book like this one to come to life, a lot of work goes into it. I would love to show my appreciation to all the people that have made this possible:

My family, for all the time they have given me to concentrate and put in the energy to make this project a reality.

My associates who I employ to help me with the hard work such as proofreading, typesetting, editing, reviewing. Design and all other aspects of the book project.

The researchers and fact checkers sho rigorously go through the book to ensure that we stay legal and avoid publishing plagiarised work.

To all the readers who take time to purchase and read these books. They have an essential message, and the aim is to leave a legacy, without the readers, there would be more books.

Most importantly to all the co-authors who have taken the time to contribute to this book. I never know what I will get when I think of a title, but the fact that you respond with enthusiasm and professionalism makes it all worthwhile. As we continue to explore critical topics in the co-authoring world, you continue to educate, share, and indeed allow others to enjoy your wisdom to that I say thank you. Special mention to all of you individually:

Angelinah Boniface
Charity Ngugi-Latz
Ali Abdoul
Clara Meierdierks
Judita Grubliene

Bernadetta Omondi
Savithri Jayaweera
Roland Burt
Lucy Oyubo

Further Reading

D iversity and inclusion are very wide subjects, as you finish reading this book. I would like to draw your attention to other books you can read as a follow up that you can continue to grow and keep your mind fresh.

THE DIVERSITY DELUSION: HOW RACE AND GENDER PANDERING CORRUPT THE UNIVERSITY AND UNDERMINE OUR CULTURE - HEATHER MAC DONALD.

A new book I found when I was researching how to frame the introduction for 'Celebrating Diversity'. The Author puts a provocative argument on the subject and how the rise of intolerance is eroding common sense. Without misrepresentation here is her Synopsis:

America is in crisis, from the university to the workplace. Toxic ideas first spread by higher education have undermined humanistic values, fuelled intolerance, and widened divisions in our larger culture. Chaucer, Shakespeare and Milton? Oppressive. American history? Tyranny. Professors correcting grammar and spelling, or employers hiring by merit? Racist and sexist. Students emerge into the working world believing that human beings are defined by their skin colour, gender, and sexual preference and that oppression based on these characteristics is the American experience. Speech that challenges these campus orthodoxies is silenced with brute force.

The Diversity Delusion argues that the root of this problem is the belief in America's endemic racism and sexism, a belief that has engendered a metastasising diversity bureaucracy in society and academia. Diversity commissars denounce meritocratic standards as discriminatory, enforce hiring quotas, and teach students and adults alike to think of themselves as perpetual victims. From #MeToo mania that blurs flirtations with criminal acts, to implicit bias and diversity compliance training that sees racism in every interaction, Heather Mac Donald argues that we are creating a nation of narrowed minds, primed for grievance, and that we are putting our competitive edge at risk.

But there is hope in the works of authors, composers, and artists who have long inspired the best in us. Compiling the author's decades of research and writing on the subject, The Diversity Delusion calls for a return to the classical liberal pursuits of open-minded inquiry and expression, by which everyone can discover common humanity.

There are a lot more books on Amazon and other sites that will give you different views on the subject. For me, the other Interesting books I found include:

1. Diversify - June Sarpong
2. Diversity & Inclusion: The Big Six Formula for Success – D. A. Abrams
3. Inclusion Around the Clock: Celebrating Diversity & Inclusion with Pluribus - Isabelle Pujol
4. Demystifying Diversity: A Handbook to Navigate Equality, Diversity and Inclusion Paperback – Jiten Patel and Gamiel Yafai
5. The Inclusion Imperative: How Real Inclusion Creates Better Business and Builds Better Societies - Stephen Frost

References

Dyslexia - NHS
https://www.nhs.uk/conditions/dyslexia/

Neurodiversity as a competitive advantage
https://hbr.org/2017/05/neurodiversity-as-a-competitive-advantage

Neurodiversity Rewires Conventional Thinking About Brains
https://www.wired.com/2013/04/neurodiversity/

Self-Diversity
https://www.forbes.com/sites/sebastianbailey/2014/05/21/inclusion-begins-with-understanding-the-self/#32018972442f

Traditional diversity training goes wrong when it becomes an issue of compliance rather than culture
http://www.forbes.com/sites/sebastianbailey/2014/05/21/inclusion-begins-with-understanding-the-self/

Diversity and Self Awareness tool
https://www.albertahealthservices.ca/assets/info/hp/cdm/if-hp-ed-cdm-gen-diverse-awareness-reflection-tool.pdf

Situational Leadership and Diversity Management Coaching Skills
https://iims.uthscsa.edu/sites/iims/files/Leadership-9.pdf
Kai zen
https://bbf.ru/magazine/26/5688/

About Diverse Cultures Publishing

Founded in February 2017, Diverse Cultures Publishing is an award-winning subsidiary of Diverse Cultures Ltd based in the UK, with a worldwide reach. We are an ambitious type of independent publishers whose aim is to promote authors who would struggle to compete for traditional publishers. We offer opportunities for non-authors to become authors. We believe anyone can write and become a published author provided they receive the right type of help.

Our services are personalised and individualised; clients enjoy a service that is tailored to their needs. The founder Amina Chitembo, a creative dyslexic was for many years told she could not write or read, decided to defy the odds and challenge the norm by becoming a writer and later founding Diverse Cultures Publishing.

We work with a diverse range of people, and we are ethnically sensitive. We believe that language is varied and there is no pigeon-holed 'English' in the 21st century.

Our vision is to see everyone who has been told they can't write, to defy the odds and become a published author. We work with the imperfectly perfect!

We know that not everyone can write a whole book and market it on their own. We also love the fact that co-authoring enables you to reach more readers and teach more people than you would have otherwise done on your own.

We provide opportunities to individuals to write their own books, to publish their completed manuscripts. We also enable people to co-author short stories in our advertised titles. We work with books in the following categories:

1. Business Series
3. Diversity Series.
4. Autobiographies

CAN WE HELP YOU?

We are passionate about people becoming a published author. If you are looking for a friendly publishing company, we will be happy to help. We will help you to co-author chapters in personal and professional development books. Facilitating you sharing your knowledge and teaching what you know to help other people through the books and our International Authors and Speaker Conference.

You will also leave a legacy for future generations. Cool, right?

Come and talk to us, we are here to serve you!

We encourage and support people who want to pass on their knowledge and raise their profile, to become published authors.

Why not be one of them?

Below is are some of our titles:

1. Black Men in Denial? Challenging Social Beliefs on Black Men and Prostate Cancer, by Ali Abdoul – June 2018
2. Celebrating Diversity, Co-authored by 10 Authors – August 2018.
3. Leading: How to be your own boss! Co-authored by ten authors – September 2018.
4. Mau Mau Child Experience: Born and Raised in The Kenyan Mau Mau Uprising Era, The Autobiography of Alice Wanjikū Mangat – June 2018.

5. Profitable Teams, by Amina Chitembo – May 2018.

6. Pushing through Fear Stereotypes and Imperfect, by Amina Chitembo – December 2017.

7. The Serious Player's Decisive Business Start-up Guide, by Amina Chitembo – March 2017.

8. What Serious Executives and Business Owners Need to Know Before Hiring A High-Performance Coach, by Amina Chitembo.

You can learn more about our services at: https://www.diverse-cultures.co.uk/

Notes

REVIEW REQUEST

Firstly, thanks a million for taking time to read my book. Your reviews are important to the authors and the publisher, and as they say, there is no shame in asking for help.

If you enjoyed this book and learned something from it, you can help us in one or more of the following ways:

1. **Go online, at** www.amazon.co.uk or our website www.diverse-cultures.co.uk, write a kind review and give it a 5-star rating.
2. Buy the book as a gift for someone who could benefit from reading it.
3. Continue to grow and build the happy life and success you want.

Thank you.

Printed in Great Britain
by Amazon